HAUNTED
BURY ST EDMUNDS

T0346756

HAUNTED

BURY ST EDMUNDS

ALAN MURDIE

Frontispiece: Montague Rhodes James (1862-1936), the master of ghost story writing, who grew up at Great Livermere, near Bury St Edmunds.

First published in 2006 by Tempus Publishing

Reprinted in 2008 by
The History Press
The Mill, Brimscombe Port,
Stroud, Gloucestershire, GL5 2QG
www.thehistorypress.co.uk

Reprinted 2013

British Library Cataloguing in Publication Data.
A catalogue record for this book is available from the British Library.

ISBN 978 0 7524 4204 4

Typesetting and origination by
Tempus Publishing Limited.
Printed in Great Britain.

CONTENTS

ACKNOWLEDGEMENTS

My ambition to write a book on Bury St Edmunds was first conceived many years ago and as a result a great many people have assisted in writing it.

Firstly, I would like to particularly thank photographer Anna Pearce for her dedicated work in taking the fine pictures of Bury St Edmunds used throughout the book and the back cover photograph of Fornham Park.

Many thanks are also extended to local historian Robert Halliday for help and encouragement with research over many years and to author Stewart Evans for allowing me to reproduce many rare illustrations from his collections. Stewart Evans also kindly shared his extensive local knowledge of many of the places, characters and events concerned.

A generation of staff at the Suffolk Records Office in Bury St Edmunds and Bury St Edmunds Library have tirelessly provided help and assistance in locating rare material in their care. Staff at numerous Bury St Edmunds shops, pubs and hotels over the years have all shared their experiences; I would particularly like to thank staff at the Nutshell (long may it survive!), the Cupola House and the Angel Hotel.

Local informants – too many to mention – have also contributed information and details of their experiences or given me leads or introductions whereby first-hand testimony could be obtained. All are owed a debt of thanks and I would like to mention the following in particular: Susan Adcock, Sandra Amiss, Helga Brandt of the Theatre Royal, the late Michael Brooks, Stephen Chaplin, the late Mr and Mrs Day of Fornham St Martin, Mrs Laura Dean of Ixworth, Mrs Edna Dennehey, Mrs Beryl Dyson of Great Livermere, Mrs Janice Eldrett, Paul Foulsham, Raymond Goldsmith formerly of Fornham All Saints, the late Andrew Green, David Hardy and the late Mrs Hardy of Risby, Mrs Brenda King, Mrs Jane Kingsbury, members of the Knights of St Edmund, my grandfather, the late Frederick Mann and my great uncle, the late Arthur Mann, Mrs Joyce McColl and William McColl, Kim O'Brien, Malcolm Ramplin, Sylvia Ramplin, Wendy Moore, members of the Rougham Tower Association, the late Miss Smith of Fornham St Martin, Andrew Snowdon, and Norman and Jenny Withington.

Michelle Bird kindly helped with proof reading the early chapters of the book as did my mother, Janet Murdie; Duncan McAndrew assisted with checking and correcting historical references. Mathew Lock gave technical support. The Revd Nic Sagovsky provided a useful introduction to Cambridge University Library; Dr Tom Licence of Cambridge helped and encouraged my research there. Members and staff of the Society for Psychical Research helped with leads to many Suffolk cases. Many friends in the Ghost Club have given encouragement over the last six years and I would particularly like to mention Philip Hutchinson, Lionel Gibson, Mrs Rita Leek, the late Dennis Moyses, my sister Rosemary Murdie, Lance Railton and the late Dennis Bardens.

This book is dedicated to the memory of the late Richard Halliday (1957-1997) and to M.R. James, the greatest ghost story teller of them all.

INTRODUCTION

The ghosts of Bury St Edmunds and the surrounding district have been of interest to me ever since my childhood. I was born and grew up in the area, and so have been fortunate to know many of the stories and the places concerned with the intimacy which a local connection brings. Of course, over the generations numerous outside commentators have praised Bury St Edmunds as a fine example of an English market town. Architect Sir Alex Clifton Taylor described it as one of the finest Georgian towns in the country, overlaying the unique pattern of medieval streets and buildings, themselves laid out according to principles of sacred geometry in the Middle Ages. Similarly, poet Sir John Betjamen urged visitors to see the town before developers and planners ruined it – fortunately he did not live to see his prophecy being depressingly fulfilled. But the power of Bury St Edmunds lies in more than its lengthy history and attractive architecture, and is greater than the ancient Abbey monuments and Georgian buildings which those with any sensitivity can appreciate. Bury St Edmunds and the surrounding area are places of deep spiritual significance, both within East Anglia and in Great Britain as a whole, and a belief in ghosts is an aspect of this deeper pattern.

I realise it was my good fortune to have been born at the tail-end of a village community which was comprised, in part, by people who had grown up before the First World War. The characters and personalities of this now-vanished generation had been shaped by a primarily agricultural pattern of life, with a result that they had a very different outlook to the materialistic one of the later twentieth century. Although few had been formally educated beyond their early teens, their language and experience of life had not been dulled by the mass media. They preserved stories and treasured traditions which had been handed down from earlier generations.

Whilst their vision of the world may have been a smaller one, it was a more vivid one than that conveyed second-hand through computer and television screens. Furthermore, it was a vision that readily acknowledged ghostly presences and the next world. Listening to the colourful old dialect of otherwise wholly down-to-earth individuals in my early years, I found that many of them had a real and matter-of-fact acceptance of ghosts as part of a greater spiritual realm. To them local places were not simply parcels of land or plots awaiting development, but haunted places with stories of phantoms which might be encountered after dark. These Suffolk natives believed in ghosts for the most compelling of reasons – either they or their families had direct experience of them.

This picture of a deeper pattern underlying reality had been recognised by earlier generations as encompassing the whole town of Bury St Edmunds. Still possessing some the most impressive monastic remains in Great Britain, Bury St Edmunds was considered one of the most holy spots in the whole of England. Indeed, its very existence is derived from faith in St Edmund, martyred in the name of Christ and the original patron saint of all England. Belief in the power of God and his Saint still has a strong resonance in the town and reverberates across time into the twenty-first century.

The graves of the former abbots of St Edmund's Abbey uncovered in excavations in 1902–03.

Of course, some of the ideas that have been inspired by the spiritual and psychic side of Bury St Edmunds are fanciful – for instance, that it lies on the path of an enormous ley line known as St Michael's Ley or that the signs of the zodiac are laid out in features of the countryside around. However, there is no doubt about its continuing significance as a spiritual centre, even if that power has seemed dormant to many.

Against this backdrop Bury St Edmunds and its environs may be considered a haunted area, both metaphorically and literally. Whilst it has not been possible to include every story or experience, it is hoped the selection which follows will give as comprehensive a summary of the spectral residents of the town and its environs as is possible in the space available. *Haunted Bury St Edmunds* seeks to permanently record many of these experiences and beliefs for the first time in book form.

Chapter one considers the ghosts of monks, and manifestations of St Edmund's power up to the present day and to which many will testify. Chapter two examines the most famous Bury St Edmunds ghost story, the legend of the Grey Lady which has enthralled generations. Chapter three looks at two local murders where the killers received final justice in execution in Bury St Edmunds, but left a legacy of ghostly tales behind them. Chapter four examines accounts of hauntings in a number of different premises around the town and Chapter five surveys a selection of stories from surrounding villages. The final chapter looks at how life and art have interwoven with the ghosts of the village of Great Livermere, north of Bury St Edmunds. It is a fitting piece of synchronicity that a village which is a candidate for the title of 'the most haunted village in England' also turns out to have been the childhood home of Montague Rhodes James (1862-1936) who wrote what are undoubtedly the finest fictional ghost stories in the English language.

Where appropriate I have commented upon the nature of phenomena from the perspective of the theories and data accumulated by scientific psychical research. However, I believe no single explanation can account for all ghost experiences, and with the ghosts of Bury St Edmunds many mysteries remain.

ONE

THE SACRED TOWN OF BURY ST EDMUNDS AND ITS MONASTIC GHOSTS

To walk amongst the majestic ruins of St Edmund's Abbey in Bury St Edmunds is to walk upon some of the most holy soil in the whole of England. As a town, Bury St Edmunds possesses some of the most impressive monastic remains in the whole of Great Britain, the surviving parts of the great Abbey of St Edmund. Rivaling Glastonbury Abbey in size and power, St Edmund's Abbey was an enormous Benedictine centre, the shrine of the martyred Saint and King Edmund, and one of the most important pilgrimage sites in Western Europe.

So holy was the soil of Bury St Edmunds considered in the Middle Ages that English monarchs would dismount to walk the last mile, entering the town along the old processional route from the west, still known as King's Road. Over the centuries, in the heart of the Abbey, thousands of pilgrims joined the community of monks engaged in worship, contemplation and prayer to commune with God and the life beyond. For over 500 years, the relics of St Edmund, King and martyr, were preserved and venerated as one of the most powerful saints of the Middle Ages.

Surrounding the Abbey, the street plan of the medieval centre of the town was laid out according to a sacred plan, symbolising the medieval view of the structure of the universe. At its heart was the Abbey representing heaven, next came the realm of angels, known to this day as Angel Hill, then spreading beyond it was the earth, the secular town of man's domain with the streets set out upon a grid pattern. Finally, there came the wall and the town ditch as a perimeter and beyond it lay the area representing hell, extending over what later became Bury cattle market and beyond. Here was the place where rubbish and the bodies of outcasts were abandoned, and tradition holds that potential plague-carriers were required to wash their coins in a stone font that can be still seen on Risbygate Street (in fact, it is the base of a cross shaft).

The monks were not only busy above ground, but also beneath it, constructing tunnels, catacombs and chambers. It is not surprising that such an area may be considered haunted and throughout the medieval heart of the town there have been many reports of ghosts over the last 100 years. But it should be noted that the first apparition reported in the town was that of St Edmund himself, and a very powerful and dangerous one he could prove, slaying marauding kings, helping rout armies and punishing those who desecrated his shrine.

ST EDMUND'S HEAD.

Left: *St Edmund, King and martyr, guarded his shrine, town and people.*

Opposite: *The site of the High Altar of the Abbey which many find a spiritually charged spot.*

The Avenging Ghost of St Edmund

Before his death, Edmund was a Christian King of East Anglia, a man of remarkable piety and faith. He refused to enter into treaties with the invading Danes unless they converted to Christianity. No more than thirty years of age, he stood in defiance against a far larger force of Danes sweeping into the kingdoms of eastern England, and refused any compromise or surrender to them. Against great odds his small army went into battle, and was defeated near Thetford in November 869.

Soon after, King Edmund was himself captured by his heathen enemies. Steadfastly refusing to renounce his faith or his kingdom, the Danes executed him on 20 November 869. Historians have differed as to the site of his martyrdom; candidates proposed for the site include Hellesdon near Norwich and Bradfield St George, south of Bury St Edmunds, whilst Suffolk tradition has long averred that it took place at Hoxne. Tying Edmund to a tree, they fired volleys of arrows into his body and then decapitated him, casting his body and severed head into a thicket. With this act of mutilation, the Danes no doubt believed that both Edmund and the faith he stood for had been extinguished as a power in the region. But the martyred King Edmund was to more than amply demonstrate the adage that nations which go down fighting rise again.

After the Danes had moved on, Edmund's surviving followers sorrowfully searched the thick woods for days for his body. On the point of abandoning their search, they heard a voice calling,

10

'Here! Here! Here!' and on reaching the spot found Edmund's severed head in a thicket of thorns, miraculously guarded by an enormous wolf. On their arrival the friendly wolf picked up the head and led the searchers to where the body lay and then loped off into the woods, 'with doleful mourning'. The followers of Edmund then placed the severed head next to the torso and thereupon witnessed a further wonder, when the head and body were miraculously reunited. Later chronicles tell that the neck showed merely a line like 'a purple thread' indicating where the severed parts had been reconnected.

In this miraculous state of preservation, the body of Edmund was initially guarded by volunteers and later moved to the small town of Bedoricksworth which occupied the site of present-day Bury St Edmunds. Here the first shrine was established, maintained by ordinary people. At various points the remains of the saint were moved but eventually it was returned to the town and a permanent shrine established with ecclesiastical support. It was around the shrine that what is today Bury St Edmunds grew up.

Once a year the incorrupt body was washed and the hair combed. It was said the hair and nails continued to grow and that these were clipped and preserved as relics. Undoubtedly, the miraculous preservation of the body intensified the belief that St Edmund remained potent on the spiritual level. His apparition was believed to appear at times of danger, or manifest in dreams to issue warnings. In other cases he would appear and strike down those who sought to despoil his shrine or lands.

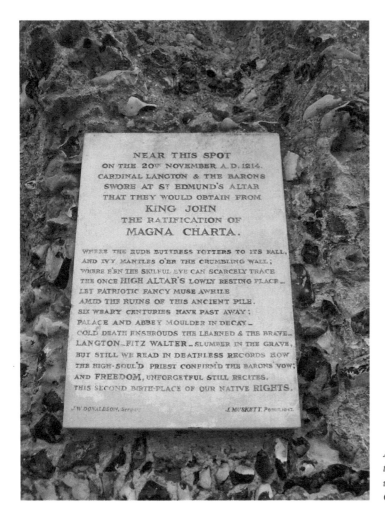

NEAR THIS SPOT
ON THE 20™ NOVEMBER A.D. 1214.
CARDINAL LANGTON & THE BARONS
SWORE AT ST EDMUND'S ALTAR
THAT THEY WOULD OBTAIN FROM
KING JOHN
THE RATIFICATION OF
MAGNA CHARTA.

WHERE THE RUDE BUTTRESS TOTTERS TO ITS FALL,
AND IVY MANTLES O'ER THE CRUMBLING WALL;
WHERE E'EN THE SKILFUL EYE CAN SCARCELY TRACE
THE ONCE HIGH ALTAR'S LOWLY RESTING PLACE.
LET PATRIOTIC FANCY MUSE AWHILE
AMID THE RUINS OF THIS ANCIENT PILE.
SIX WEARY CENTURIES HAVE PAST AWAY;
PALACE AND ABBEY MOULDER IN DECAY.
COLD DEATH ENSHROUDS THE LEARNED & THE BRAVE.
LANGTON. FITZ WALTER. SLUMBER IN THE GRAVE,
BUT STILL WE READ IN DEATHLESS RECORDS HOW
THE HIGH-SOUL'D PRIEST CONFIRM'D THE BARONS' VOW;
AND FREEDOM, UNFORGETFUL STILL RECITES,
THIS SECOND BIRTH-PLACE OF OUR NATIVE RIGHTS.

J.W DONALDSON, Sculpt.   J. MUSKETT. Posuit 1847.

A plaque commemorating the oath sworn by the Barons which led to the Magna Carta.

The most celebrated occasion was in 1014 when he slew the Danish King Sweyn Forkbeard, father of King Canute. Medieval accounts celebrated how the tyrant Sweyn:

> ... dared to exact a heavy tribute from the town where lies the uncorrupted body of the royal martyr, a thing that no-one had dared to do before ... he repeatedly threatened, also, that if he was not quickly paid, he would burn the town, together with the townsmen, utterly destroy the Church of the Martyr himself, and torment the clergy with various torture.'

Not content with extortionate threats, Sweyn was prepared to make even more reckless and insulting statements. As the chroniclers recorded, '... he even dared to speak slightingly of the martyr himself' and – what sealed Sweyn's fate – 'to say there was no saint at all'.

Supernatural retribution was swift. Towards the evening of the same day, before a crowd of Danes, Sweyn beheld the apparition of St Edmund coming towards him. Sweyn began to shriek, exclaiming, 'Fellow soldiers, to the rescue, to the rescue! Behold St Edmund has come to slay me'. But only Sweyn could perceive the apparition which proceeded to pierce him with a javelin as he sat upon his throne. Collapsing from his seat, Sweyn writhed in torment until nightfall and after three days, 'terminated his life by a shocking death.' Plans to tax Bury St Edmunds were immediately abandoned and as the Revd Richard Yates put it in his work *The History and Antiquities of the Abbey of Bury St Edmunds (1843)* thereafter, 'The supernatural powers of the Royal Saint and martyr were therefore Blazoned with unceasing exertion.' King Edward the Confessor wisely granted the liberty of St Edmund, and the abbot was recognised not simply as a pastor and father to his community, but also lord of the town of Bury St Edmunds. As a result the abbot held a seat as a peer in parliament and provided knights to fight for the king in times of war.

The wealth and power of the Abbey were constantly enriched by a stream of pilgrims from all over England and from abroad. Many healing miracles were attributed to St Edmund who was the patron saint of all England before the promotion of St George in the reign of Richard I. But these beliefs co-existed with a continuing recognition of the saint as an instrument of divine vengeance. There is no doubt that his wrath and curse were considered among the most potent in the Middle Ages, capable of bringing the most powerful in the land to repentance. The effects of St Edmund's wrath brought death, insanity, venereal disease and destruction of property, well documented in medieval literature.

St Edmund did not distinguish between classes and rank. He had no hesitation in blasting impiety on the part of the high and mighty as much as that of any common thief. On one occasion a nobleman named Leofstanus, presuming to doubt the incorruption of the martyr's body, ordered the saint's tomb opened before him. Immediately, he saw the uncorrupted body and repented his action but, 'being seized by a demon, miserably expired.' In another version, Leofstanus was an abbot who similarly and rashly expressed a lack of faith over the preservation of the body and was smitten by a stroke. In later demonstrations of power, St Edmund was considered responsible in helping rout the army of the rebellious Earl of Leicester at the Battle of Fornham in 1173. No doubt mindful of this event, just over forty years later, the barons seeking to curb the power of King John deliberately chose the high altar of St Edmund's Abbey to swear their oath to introduce the Magna Carta.

The power of the saint would also manifest within the precincts of the Abbey itself. When thieves broke into the Abbey hoping to find easy plunder from the golden and jewelled shrine they were paralysed by the power of the saint as they climbed on ladders, and were thus easily captured by the bodyguard of the Abbey. On another occasion a woman conceived the idea of stealing offerings with her mouth by feigning to kiss the table on which offerings were made. But on attempting to put her plan into action she found her lips fastened to the table.

The power of St Edmund reigned supreme until the Reformation overthrew all monastic institutions under the reign of King Henry VIII. The Abbey was surrendered to the forces of the Crown on 4 November 1539 and sold into private hands. The last abbot, John Reeve, was offered a pension by the King but refused to take a penny of the royal bribe. He moved into a house on the site of the Dog & Partridge pub close to his beloved Abbey and died the following year.

One of the last historic victims of the curse was generally regarded as King Henry VIII for the instigation of the dissolution of the monasteries. King Henry reputedly died in agony crying, 'The monks, the monks'. Ecclesiastical curses also fell upon wealthy families who took over confiscated monastic lands or converted religious houses into secular dwellings. It seems that the abbot's palace proved a less than satisfactory domestic property over the years for it was entirely demolished by 1720, whilst a local banker named John Spink, who acquired an Abbey chapel in the eighteenth century, suffered the failure of his bank.

The Abbey Gateway in the early nineteenth century.

Ghost Monks in the Town

Although the last monks were driven from the Abbey in 1539, their presence has not faded from the town. For over a century there have been reports of phantom monks appearing in the area around the centre. In 1902 excavation work took place in the cathedral churchyard and the graves of a number of the abbots were discovered and opened. The following year the Cambridge medieval scholar and ghost story writer M.R. James (see Chapter six) undertook an excavation of the chapter house, discovering a number of important artefacts now preserved in Moyses Hall Museum in Bury St Edmunds. Interestingly, it seems that it was following these excavations that the first reports of ghost monks began to circulate.

In 1978 the late Mrs Copeland of Fornham St Martin recalled that phantom monks had been seen in her childhood home in Hatter Street in the early 1900s. She remembered servants going in dread of night-time encounters with ghost monks, and a number of the family's staff had given notice after being terrified by their experiences. It was believed that the ghost monks were moving along the route of old tunnels, long said to lie beneath the centre of the town which bisected the cellars of properties in many of the oldest streets.

In 1942 veteran ghost hunter Peter Underwood was stationed near Bury St Edmunds as a young soldier. During his time in the town he heard several stories of people seeing monks

The interior of the Abbey Gate where a phantom monk has been seen. (from an illustration by G.E. Chambers)

around the great Abbey Gateway, close to the structure itself. One of the finest preserved monastic structures in England, it is no mere grandiose entrance but also an imposing fortification, complete with battlements, a portcullis and arrow slits. These fortifications were considered necessary, previous gateways having been destroyed in riots by the townspeople in 1327 and 1347.

From the beginning of the 1960s, the ghostly monks acquired the general nick-name of 'the Brown Monk'. Over the years there have been claims that he has been seen in the cellar of the Cupola House in the Traverse and in the basement of the now closed Suffolk Hotel on the Buttermarket. One vague local story holds that he is the ghost of a monk who was trapped or lost in the underground tunnels, but accounts of apparitions from these two sites indicate a haunting by a female presence (usually identified as the Grey Lady and detailed in Chapter two) rather than a monk. The majority of sightings of a monk concentrate around the Abbeygate Street area, and may involve more than one figure. They have also been given the general name 'the Brown Monk', in spite of the fact that the robes of the Benedictine monks of St Edmund's Abbey were black.

Author and retired local police officer, Stewart Evans, attributes the name of the Brown Monk to a series of pranks in the late 1950s when a police officer dressed in a brown robe and strode through the cathedral churchyard, to give the impression of a haunting in the area.

A solitary apparition known as the 'Brown Monk' has been seen in many parts of old Bury St Edmunds.

If so, this would not be the first time a hoax led to a fictitious identity being given to a genuine apparition, the same process having occurred with the Grey Lady. However, a reference to a monk in brown robes occurred in a séance communication as early as 1944 (see below). It is possible that the name may also owe something to the sighting which was reported in May 1961 by Mr E. Walton who had seen a monk in brown clothing standing in the cellar of his shop. When washing his hands something brushed his shoulder. Turning around Mr Walton saw a monk, which he described as an elderly man with a drawn face. Mr Walton stated, 'He was standing there, dressed in a brown habit. His arms were akimbo, and his smile enigmatic. He just looked at me. I could not move or speak.'

The monk watched Mr Walton, then glided away and disappeared. Reporting the story, the *Bury Free Press* also quoted Mrs Rush, who ran a women's outfitters further along Abbeygate Street, and believed her premises to be haunted by a Grey Lady. Her ex-business partner had seen a ghostly monk who would appear and disappear in the door. Nobody had believed her when she told them about the ghosts, and she hoped that people would believe her now, following Mr Walton's account.

The following month the *Bury Free Press* ran a front-page story about two men who had seen the transparent outline of a monk's habit standing in Angel Lane. It had moved along the lane, and gone through a wall into the rear of Westgate & Sons, where Mr Walton had seen the monk. Interest in ghosts grew, and the following week somebody said he had been walking down

Churchgate Street near the entry to Angel Lane at 1 a.m., near a cigarette vending machine, when he heard a coin being inserted and the slot opening and shutting although there was nobody by the machine.

The stories prompted several ghost hunts by both journalists and teenagers. Two press reporters spent a night in Westgate & Sons. They were alarmed to hear a noise coming down the stairs, but it was only the office cat. In June two teenagers attempted an all-night vigil in Angel Lane, and at 2.30 a.m. they did see a mysterious shadow by the side of Westgate & Sons, although this had vanished when they reached the spot.

Interest in ghosts revived the following February, when two motorists saw the brown monk hovering in Churchgate Street. The following week a local man said that he had been driving past the Old Gaol in Southgate Street on his way to Sudbury, when he saw a monk in a brown habit, which stood still for two seconds before disappearing through the jail wall.

A Monk at the Norman Tower

Two sightings of a hooded figure have occurred near the Norman Tower, a four-storeyed bell tower next to St James Cathedral and the old West Front of the Abbey. A metal statue of St Edmund has stood in the grounds since 1974. In 1966, Mary Anderson, a native of Bury St Edmunds who had moved to Huntingdon, paid a return visit to her home town. She parked her car in the churchyard, behind the Norman Tower, before walking into the town. On her return she looked towards the West Front of the Abbey where she saw a cloaked figure moving towards the cathedral, 'The figure was human- like in its appearance, but nevertheless moved far too gracefully for any man or woman on this earth.' Mary wanted to call out, but found herself unable to speak. When she told her friends they laughed at her, but she was certain that she had seen something unusual, and, despite the risk of ridicule, she felt compelled to contact the local press with the details.

In February 2000 a local lady contacted me to relate that she had seen a hooded figure gliding in the undercroft of the Norman Tower, which is below the modern street level. She identified the figure with stories of the Grey Lady (see Chapter two) and the Abbey's ghosts and thought that it had some kind of spiritual significance. As she did not see any face, its description could match that of any figure in robes with a hood, so it could have represented a monk

Sightings near the Abbey Gateway

Over the last forty years, sightings of the ghost monk seem to have been concentrated in the area around the Abbey Gateway and Abbeygate Street. One morning in September 1967, Mr Peter Hearn, a thirty-seven-year-old carpenter, was at work in the cellar of the Wine Vaults in Abbeygate Street when he saw a figure pass by him and disappear. At first he thought this might have been another workman or a prowler, but he found that all the other people working in the building had been upstairs. Peter Hearn may have been susceptible to visions, having previously seen an apparition on the main road between Bury St Edmunds and Rougham. Local oral accounts of the story, still current, aver that an alsatian dog taken down into the cellar reacted in fear as if responding to an invisible presence.

On Bonfire Night 1970 David Hardy, then a ten-year-old boy, attended a firework party held in the gardens of the Barclays Bank in Abbeygate Street. Looking up at the upstairs window of

Left: *The undercroft of the Norman Tower.*

Opposite: *A ghostly monk has been inside buildings in Abbeygate Street.*

an old cart and coach house he saw a hooded figure appearing behind the glass, its face covered by a shadow. The building was empty at the time and was later demolished. The figure was visible for about five seconds before disappearing.

In July 1975 Dennis Taylor, a forty-seven-year-old hairdresser, reported that he had been driven out of his Hatter Street shop by an apparition. The story reached the local press, and a frightened Mr Taylor was pictured by both the *East Anglian Daily Times* and the *Bury Free Press*. He unburdened his feelings of a presence in the shop, stating, 'When I'm alone there's this terrible feeling and I just have to get out. It is as if something was coming at me all the time.'

Mr Taylor had recently seen the ghost as he was lying in bed upstairs. He described it as a faceless figure, 'It was about 5ft high and mostly monk shape. It moved towards me and I moved very sharply out.' He believed that the ghost turned on the taps in his shop. On another occasion he reported that the ghost had physically thrown him out of his shop as he cashed up on his own one night. He might have preferred to leave his business, but he was unable to as he held it on a long lease.

Three months later, in October 1975, a ghostly monk was reported in Annabel Togs Boutique in Abbeygate Street. Mrs Sandra Ovenden, a shop assistant, claimed to have seen the figure of a monk walk through the wall in the direction of Abbeygate Street as she opened the shop. Mrs Ovenden said the figure walked across from the counter and just carried on through the wall.

The figure, which glided rather than walked, was about 5ft 7ins tall, in a brown habit with a pointed hood. Mrs Ovenden added that she often heard noises upstairs, and that other shop workers would only go to the upstairs stockroom in pairs, and preferred to use the public conveniences rather than the shop's toilets. However, she insisted, 'He is not hostile. You can tell because there's an atmosphere. It's difficult to understand because people are so sceptical. We hear noises above. He often walks across upstairs.'

I visited the shop a few days after the reports were published and was told that the monk had been gliding in the direction of the Abbey Gateway. Staff speculated that the ghost may have moved upstairs or into a cellar whilst continuing his walk. The appearance coincided with the discovery of a deep shaft in the basement of a shop not far away in Churchgate Street and one local man, armed with a camera, spent all night in the shaft hoping to capture a picture of the ghost. Shortly afterwards, Malcolm Rampling of the East Anglian Psychical Research Unit organised an all-night vigil in the shop, but nothing occurred.

Former Bury police officer Stewart Evans recalled an experience one night in 1974 or 1975. It is difficult now to imagine just how dark the centre of Bury St Edmunds was during the

1970s when street lamps were only kept on in the town until about 1 a.m. Stewart Evans recalls the Angel Hill on some nights as a 'pool of blackness', with the main light coming from an illuminated column of a road sign known affectionately as 'the Pillar of Salt'. One night at about 2 a.m., Stewart Evans was on car patrol around the town and met an officer on foot patrol on the Angel Hill. Exchanging greetings, they stood speaking by the Pillar of Salt when both glimpsed a figure to right of the gateway, moving into the corner where the gateway meets the old wall of the Abbey. The figure appeared to be running and, 'we both saw it from the peripheral vision and turned round to look simultaneously. We were convinced it was a person. We both asked each other if we had seen it and hastened over to near the gateway, expecting to find someone hiding close by'. On arriving at the spot their search revealed nothing and there was no entrance for the figure to have escaped through, only the solid ancient wall. For his part, the beat officer was convinced he had seen a ghost; Stewart remains sceptical of ghosts but cannot explain what both of them perceived.

There appear to be no more reported sightings of the Brown Monk until 1985 when Mrs Leigh Baxter, now residing in the United States, saw an apparition in the Abbey Gardens. At the time of her sighting, Mrs Baxter was a teenager. She recalls going into the park after dark with three similarly aged friends who between them comprised two couples, with amusement and romance on their minds rather than any intention of ghost hunting. All of them witnessed a lone hooded figure standing in the park, but they were convinced it was not a living human being. Fearing that they would get into trouble as much as any encounter with a ghost, they left the scene in a hurry and did not report their sighting to anyone at the time.

In 1992 a phantom monk appeared in the now-closed Fleetwood's Bar, an upstairs drinking club on the corner of Abbeygate Street and Lower Baxter Street. At 1.30 a.m., after closing the bar to the public, Charlie Brueton, the manager, reported seeing a monk-like apparition which took some steps towards him and then vanished. About an hour and a half later the ghostly image reappeared, at which point Charlie said, 'the place felt like a freezer'. Charlie Brueton added that during the night that the monk appeared, a crate of Newcastle Brown beer had moved about 8ft from one part of the bar to another. Inspired by his experiences, Charlie claimed to have stayed up the next night, hoping to witness the ghost again, but his experiment proved no more successful than other previous overnight vigils in the area. He discussed the sighting with many people, some of whom had been genuinely interested, and others who treated it as a joke. Previously sceptical, he said he now believed in ghosts.

Occasional reports continue to surface of activity in Abbeygate Street. For example, in 2000 a local pamphlet on ghosts published by the curator of the Manor House Museum, reported that a ghostly monk had been glimpsed in the Baker's Oven shop in Abbeygate Street but details were sparse. In mid-January 2006 staff at a jeweller's shop at the end of Abbeygate Street told me that they believed a ghost monk was to blame for a strange smell, strange noises and the feeling of presence encountered on a staircase.

The Ghost of the Last Abbot?

What may have been an appearance of the last abbot of St Edmunds Abbey (or possibly a bishop) was a figure seen in 1993 by a lady named Mrs Vida Rasche, who was then living in a house in Crown Street. Her house was close to the Dog & Partridge pub which was traditionally said to be the home of John Reeve, the last abbot of Bury St Edmunds. One night, between 11 p.m.

The Dog & Partridge pub, said to have been the home of the last Abbot.

and midnight, she was sitting up in bed when she saw a middle-aged male figure in ecclesiastical robes move through the room. The figure was wearing what appeared to be a mitre on its head, and seemed partially illuminated before fading away. Her husband was unable to see the apparition. There are vague rumours of a haunting at the Dog & Partridge pub, and unexplained footsteps were reported by a member of staff in early 2006.

Reviewing the sightings of monks, it may be noted that few are reported as appearing within the former Abbey precincts which became a public park in 1907. Rather, the majority arise from inside buildings forming part of the medieval streets complex outside. This may be because the Abbey Gardens are only open to the public during the day and normally closed at night. Changes in brain chemistry between day and night seem to result in increased psychic sensitivity and it has tended to be people late at night or early in the morning who have reported experiences. Sightings of the phantom monk appear to come in cycles, and it may be noted that the monk is always referred to as a solitary apparition; there are no accounts of groups of monk-like figures appearing in processions as occur at a number of other haunted sites, other than a vague tradition at Fornham Priory (see Chapter two). Another characteristic is that the

A portrait of Philip Webling produced by a psychic artist which bore a strong resemblance to his living twin brother Paul (opposite).

monk is seen when people are not expecting him, whilst deliberate vigils held in the hope of an experience do not meet with success.

Taken collectively, if the bulk of the sightings of phantom monks are all treated as genuine, it may be noted that no one theory about ghosts seems to provide a satisfactory explanation. For example, one theory popular amongst many researchers is that mental images may be impressed upon the environment, like a recording on video tape. Such ideas underlie the so-called 'stone tape' or 'place-memory theory' of ghosts. This postulates that energy is imprinted upon substances such as stone and replayed at intervals in the form of a ghostly image. Such manifestations lack consciousness and cannot interact with human observers. Of course, ancient stone is in abundance in the heart of Bury St Edmunds, but there is no evidence that stone or any other substance behaves like a tape recorder. The term is best considered no more than a metaphor or analogy for certain aspects of psychic experience, for much also seems to depend on the sensitivity of a particular individual witness. It is noticeable that in some cases, observers have felt that the ghostly monk was conscious of their presence and seemed to react to them; two of the reports also mention object movements nearby. This might suggest the presence of either a spirit or some complex hallucinatory process involving extra-sensory perception of earlier times and places, perhaps the mental states of long-dead monks, together with the release of some kind of psychokinetic energy. Yet if the phantom monks represent spirits of the dead, why is no more convincing effort made to communicate?

Paul Webling.

Communications from former Monks

One enduring mystery is the fate of St Edmund's body and relics after the dissolution of the Abbey. Possible clues to the whereabouts of the relics were sought from psychic sources, by a local clergyman, the Revd Archie Frederic Webling who was rector of Risby, a village four miles north-west of Bury St Edmunds, between 1926 and 1950. The Revd Webling wrote several books on local history and a well reviewed historical novel *The Last Abbot,* concerning the dissolution of Bury Abbey. What was not initially revealed to the public was that material in this latter book had been obtained through séances with which the Revd Webling had been involved since 1932. Hints of this appeared in a book he wrote on the history of his parish, *Risby* (1945), in which he stated:

> I am persuaded that the essential facts, credibly attested, are available. The existence of a world of spirit-life into which we pass at the death of the earth-body, our status therein being conditioned by the character we have developed here, are to those who are acquainted with the evidence no longer matters of belief but knowledge.

But the full story only emerged when in 1948 he published a book detailing sittings with mediums, which shed light on the history of the Abbey and the fate of St Edmund's remains.

*The statue of St Edmund,
cathedral churchyard.*

It seems that the Revd Webling was partly inspired to explore mediumship by the work of Frederick Bligh Bond at Glastonbury, who early in the twentieth century had used psychic means in an attempt to discover information about Glastonbury Abbey, and who subsequently conducted archaeological digs on the details obtained. (Bligh Bond later lost his job as a church architect, partly as a result of these unorthodox research techniques.) But a far more personal and compelling influence upon the Revd Webling was the loss of his twin sons. One named Philip died in infancy whilst the other called Paul died whilst serving with the RAF at Malta in January 1943.

From 1932 onwards, the Revd Webling believed he had made occasional contact with the spirit of Philip at séances. Without prior knowledge, a psychic artist produced a portrait which showed his son Philip in spirit form, appearing as a young man in his twenties. This was considered to closely resemble his then living twin brother Paul. The Revd Webling hung the portrait in his study, and later transcripts of séances suggest that he considered the expression on the picture would appear to change when the spirit of Philip would contact him or influence his thoughts through a form of telepathy. In addition to messages from his sons, the

Revd Webling believed that, via mediums, he reached out to dead monks from Bury Abbey who wished to share knowledge about its past, which had been lost since the Reformation. It is among these messages that a reference to a monk in brown robes first appears in 1944. Another alleged communicator was the Revd Stainton Moses, an Anglican clergyman who later became a celebrated spiritualist medium before his death in 1892.

As with all spiritualist communications, the source of these messages is an open and ultimately unanswerable question. The hypothesis that the messages are derived from discarnate spirits of the deceased, is not capable of being proved with total certainty. The question of proof is complicated by the possibility that such communications may be products of the unconscious mind of the medium, which may use genuinely mysterious abilities of telepathy or clairvoyance to obtain information. As with most mediumistic communications there was little which could be verified or proved to be beyond the knowledge of either the medium or the persons present at the séance. The Revd Webling was alert to this possibility but was personally convinced that he had indeed contacted his sons in the afterlife; certainly his claims were met with interest and sympathy. It seems that in the period both before and after the Second World War both the Church of England and the public in general were more open to serious psychical research. Widespread interest had been stimulated by Harry Price and his investigations at Borley Rectory, not far away on the Suffolk/Essex border, and many clergymen were prepared to talk publicly about their own experiences. The Revd Webling was in fact one of a number of Anglicans who believed themselves to have been in touch with the spirits of former monks during the 1940s and 1950s (others included the Revd Bradshaw and his wife at Elm, near Wisbech in Cambridgeshire). Certainly, his views do not seem to have been a bar to his ministry locally, for in 1947 he was made an honorary canon of St Edmundsbury Cathedral, a position he held until retiring to Horndean in Hampshire in 1950.

Among many extraordinary claims, he learned that Bury St Edmunds shared a link with Iona and that the glory of St Edmund's Abbey still existed upon the spiritual plane. Perhaps most remarkable were messages that the final burial place of St Edmund still lay within the Abbey, awaiting rediscovery. When these stories emerged in 1948, his claims were treated with serious interest by the local press.

Certainly, mysteries remain as to the whereabouts of the bones of St Edmund's body following the dissolution of the monastery. One story held that they were stolen in the reign of King John and taken to Toulouse where they were exhibited for several hundred years before disappearing at the time of the French Revolution. Identified again in the nineteenth century, the alleged bones (with the exception of the skull) were brought to England in 1901 and taken under the care of the Catholic peer the Duke of Norfolk. The bones were interred at Arundel Castle in Sussex, where they remain today but when examined some years ago by specialists it was concluded that they came from a number of different individuals, and probably included more than one woman. This finding strengthens the case that the remains of the saint never left the Abbey, a view endorsed by M.R. James, and the possibility remains that they are concealed somewhere beneath the ruins of the Abbey.

The Power of St Edmund Invoked Again

Little mention was made of the spiritual communications and the sacred side of Bury St Edmunds for nearly sixty years, until plans for major redevelopment in the town were raised. However, in the twenty-first century, the power of St Edmund and his curse has become a potent local issue again, revived at the end of 2005 in a battle against plans to redevelop the town centre and the construction of a giant shopping mall. Although there was a vote in a local referendum in December 2004 which overwhelmingly rejected the scheme, the local St Edmundsbury Borough Council decided to carry on regardless with a scheme to build a shopping mall, put forward by developers Centros Miller, part of an Edinburgh-based property company.

Aided by local councillors and officials, plans were made to drive a wedge through the market square, disrupting the sacred geometry of historic Bury St Edmunds. These was compared by a correspondent in the local press to the actions of a treacherous shepherd named Tutt who betrayed a secret passageway into nearby Thetford to the Danes at the time of the death of King Edmund, on the promise of a great reward. Once the heathen army had sacked the town, Tutt was then hanged by the Vikings, with the hill being called Tutt Hill thereafter (another example is just outside Bury St Edmunds).

Having exhausted democratic channels a group of local people formed a body known as the Knights of St Edmund in the autumn of 2005. Using an obscure section of the Book of Common Prayer known as Commination, the Knights of St Edmund conducted a formal cursing ceremony upon Debenhams, the Miller Group and Centros Miller on the Feast Day of St Edmund, 20 November. The Commination ceremony had last been conducted in 1963 by a priest in Bramber in Sussex whose churchyard had been vandalised by Satanists.

The terms of the curse were certainly impressive, 'For now is the axe taken unto the tree … let nothing ever built upon this land prosper.' Included in the prayers was the Latin, the first time it had been read since the fourteenth century, dedicated to St Edmund. In autumn 2006 a film about the curse and its impact was reported to be underway.

Various misfortunes which have affected those promoting or involved with the scheme ever since have been readily ascribed to the growing power of the curse. Amongst the most important victims claimed was Deputy Leader of the Labour Party, John Prescott, who fell from power in 2006, following the endorsement of his regional office Go East for the scheme. Even if the shopping centre is constructed, the Knights of St Edmund aver the effects of the curse will afflict all those behind the scheme and their heirs, in perpetuity. Local belief is that the curse will only be lifted if the scheme is abandoned or the shopping mall demolished and those backing the scheme repent.

Behind the campaign is an enduring and growing belief in Bury St Edmunds as a spiritual place, shared by many people. The Revd Webling stated, 'Voices that were still (or perhaps only unheeded) are heard foretelling the days when this hallowed spot will again become a focus of spiritual power, a place of pilgrimage and the latter house even exceed the former in glory.'

TWO

THE HAUNTS OF THE GREY LADY

By far the most famous of all the ghosts of Bury St Edmunds is the Grey Lady, said to be one Maude Carew who died in the fifteenth century after being implicated in a royal assassination in the town. Celebrated in folklore for generations, the Grey Lady is said to haunt no less than six different places in the town; indeed, she may be considered a collective name for any female apparition appearing within the grounds of the Abbey and the precincts of the medieval town.

The Story of the Grey Lady

According to the most popular story, the Grey Lady is the spirit of a fifteenth-century nun named Maude Carew who became involved with a conspiracy to murder Humphrey, 'the Good Duke' of Gloucester in 1447, the brother of King Henry VI.

Maude was the impressionable and naive daughter of powerful Sir William Carew and accompanied her father on a trip to an embassy in France. Here she met and fell haplessly in love with a Suffolk nobleman named Sir Roger Drury, who reputedly possessed hypnotic powers. On returning to England, Maude felt as though she had fallen under a spell for she could not rid her mind of the image of Sir Roger. Hopelessly infatuated, she sought news of Sir Roger and eventually learned gossip that he had become a monk at Bury St Edmunds. Such was her obsession that Maude was determined to follow Sir Roger. The only route available was for her to enter holy orders herself as a nun. She took the veil and became attached to Fornham Priory in Bury St Edmunds, hoping that this might bring her into contact with her unrequited love. But on entering the Priory she found herself strangely attracted to monk known as Father Bernard, a mysterious monk of St Edmund's Abbey. Father Bernard was a man renowned for his powerful intellect and his secretive ways, fulfilling the best traditions of devout monastic scholars. Father Bernard seemed to possess an indefinable charm and she felt a strange affinity with him. Although she did not realise it, Father Bernard was none other than the disguised Sir Roger Drury, who had renounced his name, title and earlier life and taken on a completely new identity.

The remains of St Saviour's Hospital where Humphrey, Duke of Gloucester, died in 1447, from an old print.

In February 1447, a parliament of nobles was convened in Bury St Edmunds. The principal business before the titled representatives was to hold the trial of Humphrey, Duke of Gloucester on treason charges before his peers. Members of the royal family arrived in Bury St Edmunds to observe the trial, including Margaret of Anjou, the Queen of England. It was to Maude's amazement that she was summoned before her Highness for a private audience. Coming before the Queen, Maude was shocked when the Queen told her that she knew the real reason for Maude's entry to the monastic world. The Queen told her that Duke Humphrey, who was awaiting trial, was an evil man, but his power was so great that he would surely be acquitted of all charges, following which he would take revenge on all those who had accused him. Father Bernard, who was to be the most important witness at the trial, would be the first and most unfortunate victim of Duke Humphrey's revenge. The gullible Maude was horrified to hear this, but an even more amazing revelation was to come. The manipulative Queen Margaret announced that Father Bernard was none other than her secret love: Sir Roger Drury! In fact, Maude had become ensnared in a devious conspiracy to murder the duke.

The Queen then told Maude that in order to avoid Humphrey's revenge he had to be assassinated. Believing that this might be the only way to save Sir Roger's life, Maude agreed to administer a poison to Duke Humphrey whilst he slept in a chamber in St Saviour's Hospital. Entry to the hospital could be effected by stealth, as a secret tunnel ran to the building from the Abbey.

On the eve of the trial, Maude gained access to St Saviour's Hospital via the tunnel and poured poison on Duke Humphrey as he slept. But as she tried to retrace her steps through the underground passage her candle blew out, and she found herself hopelessly lost. Unfortunately, in the process of seeking an escape route, Maude inadvertently exposed herself to the remains of the poison and absorbed a fatal dose. Finally she saw a light which led to chambers occupied by Father Bernard, the former Sir Roger. Staggering into his quarters, Maude confessed all to Father Bernard who was appalled when he discovered the facts and reason for the crime. Father Bernard led her back through the secret tunnels to the Abbey church and as she died he cursed her.

The sins of the malign Queen Margaret were soon considered to have caught up with her. The Queen's son, Prince Henry, died in battle soon after and her husband, Henry VI, was to be murdered, and she was to spend most of her last years in prison or in exile. In his later years, Father Bernard was said to have later repented of his cursing of Maude and wrote an account which he concealed in a cavity of the west wall of the Abbey where it lay hidden until the nineteenth century. Neither Maude or the wicked Queen could find rest after death, for every year at 11 p.m., every 24 February (the anniversary of Duke Humphrey's death), their shades would wander through the ruins of the Abbey Gardens and St Mary's churchyard. The story has been retold periodically ever since.

Alas for tradition, this melodramatic story is a glorious fiction set against actual historical events. The real authoress of the story was a romantically inclined young woman from Bury St Edmunds writing in the Victorian era. She was Miss Margaretta Greene, a member of the Greene family who established the Greene King breweries. The Greene family resided in one of the large houses which were constructed in the West Front. Margaretta's story of Maude Carew first appeared in a novella privately published in 1861, entitled *The Secret Disclosed*, loosely based on events in 1447 and historical and contemporary rumours. On 24 February 1447, Humphrey, the Duke of Gloucester was due to stand trial in Bury St Edmunds but was found dead in his bed at St Saviour's Hospital, as recorded in a plaque on the front of the building (which was restored in 1997). On entering Bury St Edmunds the duke was said to have had a premonition of his own demise. The cause of death was taken to be apoplexy but tradition said he was murdered. After a remarkably low key funeral for a man of royal birth, Humphrey was laid to rest at St Albans. Certainly, his death was considered suspicious both at the time and by later historians but nothing can be proven.

However, Maude Carew and Father Bernard are completely fictitious, as is the role ascribed to Queen Margaret in seducing the hapless nun into her plans. The inspiration for the names and the involvement of a Queen appear to have been from the tombs contained in the nearby St Mary's church which holds the tomb of Queen Mary Tudor and would have been well known to Margaretta Green. On the north side of the chancel of St Mary's is the tomb-chest monument of Sir William Carew who died in 1501, with two effigies, whilst on the south side is a similar monument to Sir Robert Drury who died in 1536. Similarly, the existence of a tunnel stretching for nearly a mile between St Saviour's Hospital and the Abbey is highly improbable.

Humphrey, Duke of Gloucester, from an Arras manuscript.

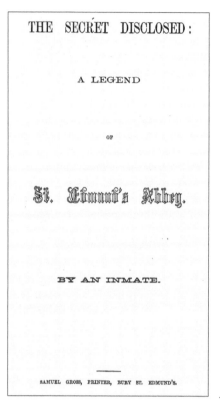

THE SECRET DISCLOSED:

A LEGEND

OF

St. Edmund's Abbey.

BY AN INMATE.

SAMUEL GROSS, PRINTER, BURY ST. EDMUND'S.

The frontispiece of Margaretta Greene's novella which helped foster stories of the Grey Lady.

The Ghost-Inspired Riot

Margaretta Greene's novella was eagerly lapped up by the local population, many of whom seemed willing to believe that every word was true, including the annual manifestations of the two ghosts. Margaretta herself was responsible for boosting belief in the supernatural, claiming it had been the sound of ghostly footsteps in her parents' house, which had first alerted her to an ancient hiding place in a wall. In this was discovered a casket containing the manuscript which inspired *The Secret Disclosed*. Such was the strength of belief that by the night of 24 February 1862 large crowds gathered around the front of Margaretta Greene's house, hoping to catch sight of the ghosts of Maude Carew and Queen Margaret.

It is quite possible that a large element of the crowd were simply there for amusement (after all, there was no television, cinema or internet to provide entertainment). However, it seems that within the crowd there were a hard core of people who genuinely believed that a manifestation was possible and whose excitement infected the others. By 11 p.m. expectancy reached a level approaching mass hysteria, and several people claimed to see two figures gliding slowly above the ground. Some said they were black, others said they were white, and others described them as, 'dark, dimly defined forms'. Others, however, began to realise it was all a hoax and the mood of the crowd became ugly. The tension was broken when people began to throw stones, some of which broke the windows in the Greene family's house. Eventually the crowd dispersed after midnight following the attendance of police. A later story, perhaps apocryphal, says that

Margaretta's nephew, John Greene, decided to entertain the ghost hunters by roaming the churchyard wearing a white sheet, only to be pelted with sticks and stones.

Such incidents of mass ghost hunting as a popular entertainment were not unknown in Victorian England; nor are these wholly extinct today. Boredom or the prospect of encountering something strange or unusual may still trigger flocks of sightseers and a mass hysteria.

Although Margaretta Greene died at a relatively early age in 1880, her story lived on. Although she is not known to have written any other books or stories, *The Secret Disclosed* had gained her a form of immortality, and her obituary said that she, 'invested the ancient Abbey ruins with a romance that has never since left them'.

Later Sightings of Maud Carew

The story of Maude Carew entered into local folklore, boosted by frequent and partial re-tellings. What is more difficult to determine is whether Margaretta based her story of a ghost on any existing tradition or took the matter wholly from her imagination. Certainly, the story has been imprinted into folk consciousness and stories of the 'Lady in Grey' or the more ubiquitous Grey Lady prowling the Abbey Gardens were known among park attendants in the 1930s; she was said to appear near a First World War tank which at one time was exhibited in the grounds (why this should exert a particular attraction remains unexplained). At least one park keeper – a veteran of the First World War and former Prisoner of War in Germany – was fascinated by the stories. He kept watch for her in the Abbey grounds on a number of occasions but without success. A further boost to the perpetuation of the story was a dramatised cinefilm version of the legend, made in same period, parts of which still survive in archives. Garbled versions of the story also appear to have been current amongst superstitious school children in Bury St Edmunds as late as the mid-1970s. One story claimed that it was death or misfortune to see her; another claimed that her ghost could be summoned by stamping three times on the bedroom floor before going to bed. The very brave attempted the ritual in the hope of experiencing a night-time encounter with the dreaded phantom, but seem to have succeeded in invoking little more than the wrath of parents, annoyed by their offspring stamping on the ceiling! Another tradition claimed that if one chanted 'Grey Lady' three times before a mirror on the night of 24 February, her ghost would appear in the glass.

But was there ever a genuine apparition? Whilst the claims of ghostly forms in the churchyard on 24 February 1862 can be attributed to mass hysteria and wishful thinking, more difficult to dismiss have been accounts of a ghostly female figure reported at no less than six different locations in the town.

St Mary's Churchyard and West Font

During the twentieth century there were stories of the Grey Lady haunting the avenue through St Mary's graveyard, where two phantom figures had supposedly been glimpsed in 1862. Whilst this tree-lined avenue is a pleasure to walk through on a summer's day, it takes on a wholly different atmosphere late on a winter's day or at night when it is largely unlit.

Nearby, the houses built into the West Front of the Abbey have long been said to be haunted by strange noises ascribed to the presence of the Grey Lady. They seem to have acquired the haunted reputation in the 1930s and 1940s when many of them became derelict and frequently

St Mary's churchyard and the area around the cathedral haunted by the Grey Lady in local tradition.

empty for long periods. A local lady, Mrs Joyce McColl, who later went on to have a first-hand experience of the Grey Lady herself (see below), recalled that in the 1940s it was considered a dare for children to go to the door of one particular empty house. Here the children would then knock and listen with excited anticipation to what were taken to be footsteps approaching the door of the abandoned house. She attempted this herself and duly heard the footsteps on one occasion but could not rule out the possibility of an echo.

Just after the Second World War, the stories were revived when the local paper reported the experiences of a former resident, Mrs Stephenson-Adams, who moved into one of the buildings during the Second World War, despite being warned that, 'it was spooky'. Once she woke up to feel something cold touching her face, but she could not turn the light on because of the blackout. On another occasion her son saw something in grey, during a party at the house. She recalled that, 'he was sitting on the Chesterfield talking to me when suddenly he said, "Did you see that?".' On being asked for details, he told his mother that, 'Something in grey passed through the room and went through the door. It looked like a shroud'. For her part, Mrs Stephenson-Adams had seen nothing but her sister had twice sensed an apparition in a downstairs room during a stay. On the first night she sensed a presence and saw a figure in brown in the room. The next night she saw the figure again, this time in grey. Each time the form vanished when she put on the light.

Strange experiences were also shared by Mrs Stephenson-Adam's daughter and a Polish officer who stayed in the house. On one occasion her daughter had sensed something in her room and screamed, with the result that her cries brought other people rushing to her aid, but again, there was nothing; to be seen. The experience of the Polish officer was more puzzling; he had awoken to the feeling of something sitting on his bed but, 'could not fathom what it was.' The account made the pages of the *Daily Express* on 1 March 1946, under the headline, 'The ghost at Mrs Adams's'.

After the Second World War, some of the properties were again sporadically inhabited but the crumbling state of the walls and general dereliction drove out many occupiers after short periods, amid continuing stories of strange sounds. On one occasion supposedly ghostly noises were discovered by builders to be attributable to birds nesting in the roof of one house; in 1950 a gas fitter humorously reported a large water stain which vaguely resembled a hooded figure appearing on the wall, 'as the image of the Grey Lady'. But little more in the way of reports were heard because the buildings were largely untenanted.

In the summer of 1983 I spoke to a retired lady who occupied one of the large, cavernous, houses close to the cathedral. An upstairs room had a splendid long table which could reputedly seat at least thirty people around it when it was used by the Church of England for meetings; another downstairs room was referred to as 'the ballroom'. The house was semi-derelict and she occupied a few rooms on the ground floor at the front. She told me that during the night she was often disturbed by strange noises which she attributed to, 'young people breaking in and running around', although she never seemed to catch any of them.

In 2006 the houses were extensively renovated and reputedly on the market at a high price. It will be interesting to see whether modernisation has finally put paid to the ghosts once and for all.

Abbeygate Street

Amid reports of ghostly monks in 1961 (see chapter one), the *Bury Free Press* also quoted Mrs Rush, who ran a women's outfitters along Abbeygate Street, who had been having her morning coffee when she heard the soft rustling of silk and the tap of heels. She stated, 'I thought it was a customer, and went out to serve her'. It was then she saw the Grey Lady. Like many female witnesses of apparitions, Mrs Rush proved a good observer of clothing, noticing that, 'She was dressed in grey chiffon and walked across the showroom to disappear through a wall. Her heels were tapping, but she was walking on carpets'. Mrs Rush stated she was 'convinced' that the appearance of the lady placed her as having been alive in the eighteenth century, 400 years after the supposed Maude Carew.

The Cupola House

The Cupola House in the Traverse is another place reputedly haunted by the Grey Lady. A comfortable town centre restaurant and bar, it was built in 1693 for an apothecary named Thomas Macro. Daniel Defoe, the author of *Robinson Crusoe,* is said to have stayed in the building (a stone plaque on the outside wall bearing his date of birth and death implies a stronger or more intimate association but this is not the case). Doubtless, Defoe would have been interested in the ghosts at the Cupola, for he was the author of a major eighteenth-century collection of true stories of the supernatural. Certainly, the property is atmospheric, being one of the tallest buildings in the old centre of Bury St Edmunds, consisting of three storeys with a fine octagonal lanthorn crowning the top. The Cupola House also possesses substantial cellars and it is these which are traditionally haunted by both the Grey Lady herself and by a ghost monk.

Cupola House in the early twentieth century. Since 2000 successive licensees and staff have reported ghostly manifestations in the building.

The latter has been variously identified as the Brown Monk (see Chapter one) or even the fictitious Brother Bernard, whose presence was claimed in a widely read article in *Psychic News* in August 1973. Not only did this repeat the fiction of Margaretta Green, but fresh repetition ensured transmission of the Maude Carew tale in books in subsequent years. In fact, there appear to be no reliable sightings of a monk recorded at the Cupola, but in recent years there have been reports of ghostly activity by successive licensees, some of which are indicative of a haunting female presence, judging by the statements from witnesses.

In 1993 licensee Roger Stone reported that a woman had been sitting in the corner of the bar and appearing in the cellars. These stories, however, may only have been received at second or third hand from regulars, and it is uncertain that Roger Stone ever saw the woman himself. But on 12 September 1993 the Cupola House was visited by local historian Robert Halliday where he spoke with a barman named Simon who told him that twice in the previous year, late at night, he and other people in the bar had seen a shape move from the building's rear entrance to the front door. Yet on both occasions the back door had been locked. He had also seen feet disappearing up the stairs, but when he looked there was nothing there. One of the other drinkers made some effort to ridicule this, but Simon seemed quite sincere.

Later licensees claimed direct experiences of phenomena themselves. Until the summer of 2000 the pub was held by Mr and Mrs Lloyd who heard strange noises in the property, particularly in the upper parts, as though furniture was being moved around and footsteps. They occurred soon after they had moved in; on one occasion Mrs Leah Lloyd believed she had also seen a strange light on the top floor and had encountered an eerie chill on the staircase.

It was during the occupancy of Mr and Mrs Lloyd that I also spoke with a bar man who wished only to be identified by his first name of Warren, whom I was told had seen a phantom lady on Sunday 20 February 2000. At the time, the license of Cupola House was shared with The Nutshell, a little further down the street. Following his experience, I was told the barman was now insisting on working only in The Nutshell, where I duly found him. Nervously smoking a cigarette as he recalled his experience three days earlier, Warren told me he had been standing at the bar and had seen a woman dressed in white on the lowest part of the stairs at about 11 p.m. No-one else could see the figure which he estimated was present for several minutes. He talked about her clothing as the costume of another age, possibly the Victorian era from his description. What had upset him most was that he did not believe in ghosts but had nonetheless seen what he could only describe as one. Warren left soon after, and a few months later the pub changed hands again.

Later that year new licensees reported manifestations. Mrs Claire Holmes believed she had encountered a presence coming down the stairs on the first floor level, on 10 October 2000. She felt as though she had walked through it, the experience being more tactile than visual but she felt it was female.

The third set of licensees, the Kingstons, arrived in 2001. Mr Peter Kingston was open minded about ghosts, believing he had seen a phantom figure himself on one occasion in his life, though not at the Cupola House. On arrival, he sensed that the place was haunted and had heard a sound like a child coughing whilst down in the cellar, which he could not trace or otherwise explain. Peter Kingston also mentioned poltergeist-like incidents including the strange failure of beer taps and pipes, which were also confirmed to me by another member of staff, who later briefly took the licence with her husband after the Kingstons, before moving elsewhere. Interference with beer barrels and the drink supply is frequently reported in allegedly haunted pubs. It may also be noted that many of these incidents occurred shortly after each new licensee arrived – which they tended to interpret as the ghost responding to a new living presence and in some way 'checking them out.'

On 21 June 2001, twelve members of the Ghost Club conducted an all-night vigil at the Cupola House. This included a series of sessions of waiting in darkness at the different levels of the property, including the hexagonal cupola which caps the top of the building – certainly a highly atmospheric location for a night-time séance! As so frequently happens on organised ghost hunts, no apparitions were seen but other possible phenomena were mentioned by participants.

Interestingly, during the evening, one member, Philip Hutchinson, reported hearing a coughing sound in the cellar, similar to the experience of Peter Kingston. An American member, Joanne Kelly, who has psychic abilities, also encountered what she felt to be a cold female presence on the staircase which made her shiver; at this stage she did not know about the history of experiences on the stairs. Not long after, the Cupola House underwent extensive renovation and repair. The building was successfully restored and has reopened as a restaurant and bar, yet has succeeded in retaining its old world charm and character.

In May and June 2006 there were reports of strange object movements in the bar, including chairs tumbling over, and on one occasion in early June 2006, a heavy fan on a window sill by

Above left: *Part of the haunted cellars beneath Cupola House.*

Above right: *The haunted staircase in Cupola House where a female apparition has been seen and felt.*

the bar fell over without obvious explanation. Staff had not heard the stories of the Grey Lady, but stated they were beginning to get the feeling that there was something unusual about the Cupola.

Suffolk Hotel

The now closed Suffolk Hotel on the Buttermarket (now the Edinburgh Woollen Mill and Waterstones bookshop) was reputedly another place frequented by the Grey Lady. Certainly, there were reports of a female apparition and presence in the hotel until 1996, but details uncovered in research suggest a modern origin for the many of the manifestations (see Chapter four). In the case of the Suffolk Hotel, the term the 'Grey Lady' provided a 'nick-name' for strange experiences and puzzling incidents which were attributed to a phantom female presence.

St Saviour's Hospital

The ruin of St Saviour's Hospital along Fornham Road and the site of Duke Humphrey's death is traditionally a scene for a haunting by the Grey Lady, although I have only received second-hand oral accounts. Bury St Edmunds fire station formerly stood in Fornham Road and one local fireman claimed sightings of a ghost around the ruin sometime in the 1970s.

A more detailed account came in 2000 from Mr Christopher Handley Howard who recalled that his grandmother Mrs Joan Seaborne had been cycling on her way to work, along Fornham Road past St Saviour's Hospital early one morning around 1966. She believed she had seen a hooded female figure, like a nun, which she took to be the Grey Lady, standing by the ruin which vanished as she cycled by. People have occasionally watched the ruin at 11 p.m. on 24 February, the anniversary of the death of Duke Humphrey, but without result. Given changes to the calendar, the failure of an apparition to appear to order is not surprising.

Houses along Fornham Road

At least two of the Victorian houses along Fornham Road have been reported as being haunted in the last fifty years, both on the same side of the road and not far from St Saviour's Hospital. In 1954 and early 1955, Mrs Joyce McColl was working as a babysitter for a family who occupied a house close to the ruin. Most people who stayed at the house considered it haunted.

Doors would open by themselves and unexplained footsteps were heard on the stairs. For their part, the family were untroubled by the phenomena and would merely remark, 'Come in Maude', when a door opened without explanation. On one occasion she heard a loud bang from upstairs, as though a body or a heavy box such as a coffin had fallen. On another occasion a male member of the family, on leave from service in the army, was awoken by the sensation of something brushing across his face – a similar report to that of a soldier at a house in the West Front some ten years before.

On one occasion, Mrs McColl awoke to see her bedroom door open. However, like the rest of the family she was not at all perturbed by the presence, which she described as, 'just a grey shape against the darkness.'

In 2000 I also received a telephone call from a lady in a building on Fornham Road who had read about the Grey Lady in an article in the local press. Unfortunately, it proved impossible to pursue the matter further because of the sensitivity of the location.

Tesco Supermarket, Fornham Road

In the years since Tesco opened a store on the site of St Saviour's Hospital, reports have circulated of members of staff being disturbed by an unseen presence. The store is open twenty-four hours a day for six days each week and phenomena initially seemed confined to the cafeteria for staff in the early hours of the morning. Certainly, the early hours of the morning between midnight and 4 a.m. provide a key time for experiencing psychic events, perhaps related to changes in brain chemistry during the night.

In May 2006 I received accounts that the location of the phenomena had moved with the relocation of the café within the store. The incidents seemed to be of a poltergeist nature, including the mysterious movement of objects and the sensation of being touched. It will be noted that these are common hallmarks of hauntings associated with pubs and places of refreshment, as demonstrated by a number of the haunted inns mentioned in this book. Unlike the disturbances in the previous cafeteria, these were not confined to the hours of darkness but were occurring when the store and canteen were open to the public. Staff had felt taps on the shoulder when no-one was present and a bowl of fruit on the shelf of a cafeteria counter was

In a house along Fornham Road the Grey Lady appeared as 'a grey shape against the darkness'.

repeatedly knocked off when no-one was nearby. On one occasion in the daytime a pile of soft drink cups had tumbled over in front of a customer without explanation.

Following these incidents, all kinds of stories had begun to spread, including uncorroborated claims that the ghost was the spirit of a young boy; others that it was a woman. The site awaits further archaeological excavation as an extension occupies part of the substantial St Saviour's site. Folklore may have a range of possible haunting spectres to select since as well as occupying the site of St Saviour's, it is also across the road from an area where a number of skeletons were discovered in 1888, believed to be linked with the chapel of St Thomas à Becket which stood nearby from the medieval period. It is also not far from the Thingoe Hill which continued to be an execution site until the end of the eighteenth century.

Fornham Priory

Travelling north along to the end of Fornham Road the traveller reaches the wall of what is now the Priory Hotel, part of the Best Western chain. Originally it was the site of the medieval Priory of St Francis, the friars being unable to build a convent in the town because of the opposition of the monks of St Edmund. After the Reformation it was used as a private house. By the start of the twentieth century there was a story that phantom monks walked along a secret tunnel

St Saviour's Hospital today and the nearby haunted Tesco supermarket.

from Fornham Priory to Bury Abbey. There is no doubt that a large amount of archaeology remains in the area, although much may have been lost in periodic flooding of the River Lark over the centuries. Certainly, the proximity of marshy ground and the river makes the presence of a tunnel unlikely.

In the 1970s, during the extension and conversion of the building from a private house, a number of skeletons were discovered. One room in the hotel is supposed to have a cold presence but staff could offer little help when members of the Ghost Club visited the hotel in September 2002.

However, an earlier tradition recorded by the *Bury Free Press* in December 1929 held the Priory was haunted by the Grey Lady, who engaged in perhaps her most bizarre and athletic manifestation. According to the story the Grey Lady would rise and float or leap over the wall of the Priory!

Although this may seem a far fetched and fragmentary tale, it remains possible that it could be based upon a garbled tradition of a genuine experience. Cases of apparitions appearing in mid-air have been recorded in a number of credible accounts collected by the Society for Psychical Research over the last 120 years and by serious researchers such as Sir Ernest Bennett in his book *Apparitions and Haunted Houses* (1939).

With some, the explanation may lay in the fact that the level of the ground has changed over the years, leaving the apparitional figure seemingly walking through thin air if the ground level is lower, or if an upper storey of a building has been demolished. Conversely there are a number of accounts of apparitions moving knee-deep through modern floors where the ground level has been raised (most famously the ghostly Roman legions seen at the Treasurer's House in York in 1953). However, in other cases the apparition appears to be closer to a symbol or idea appearing in a waking dream or vision, perhaps yielding a clue to the real nature of the Grey Lady of Bury St Edmunds.

So Who or What is the Grey Lady?

Reviewing the evidence, there is nothing to suggest that the original Grey Lady, Maude Carew, was anything other than a fictional character. Yet as this catalogue of sightings and experiences indicates there are a considerable number of people over many years who have witnessed manifestations attributed to her, although the name 'the Grey Lady' appears to have been grafted on to what may be wholly unconnected phenomena. Seeking an explanation for unexplained incidents, the term the 'Grey Lady' has provided a convenient label.

In recent years, an alternative hypothesis has been advanced for spectral White Ladies and Grey Ladies, proposing that such apparitions may be a form of archetypal hallucination, representing the *genus loci* or 'spirit of a place'.

Apparitions like Grey and White Ladies seem to be associated with particular localities such as lonely roads, old buildings, and landscapes, which trigger responses at a deep level of consciousness. Such apparitions may be connected with the more exotic female apparitions of folklore and religion, such as banshees, goddesses or angels. As such, they may be a construction of the unconscious mind stimulated by psychic forces operating both internally and externally to the brain of the witness. Such apparitions are subjective, in that they exist within the mind of the observer, but they also appear to have a degree of objective existence in that they recur at the same place to a succession of different witnesses, sometimes many years apart. The psychologist Carl Gustav Jung postulated a collective unconsciousness which was shared by humanity and containing powerful images which he termed archetypes. Jung considered, 'It not infrequently happens that the archetype appears in the form of a spirit in dreams or fantasy-products, or even comports itself like a ghost.'

Like the concept of a collective unconscious itself, these ideas must remain entirely speculative. But rather than arising from a particular deceased individual, such apparitions seem to be closer to an idea or symbol, manifesting in experiences akin to dreams and visions.

If such hypotheses have any substance, it may be that the Grey Lady of Bury St Edmunds should therefore be regarded as taking her place amongst an uncanny and ubiquitous sisterhood of Grey and White Ladies, a representative of a class of apparitions which have haunted the human mind for centuries in diverse locations.

THREE

GHOSTS AND MURDER: WILLIAM CORDER AND THE NICHOLS MURDER

Murders are thankfully rare in Suffolk. Few are remembered after more than a generation or two has passed. Yet there are two pre-Victorian murder cases whose echoes have reverberated unceasingly down the years into the twenty-first century. In both cases the law inflicted the final punishment of death, with the perpetrators all being hanged in Bury St Edmunds. Nonetheless, the memory of their atrocious crimes has lived on into the present, not only in the form of re-tellings in 'true crime' literature, but in the form of local ghost stories upon which there is no statute of limitations.

William Corder and the Murder in the Red Barn

Undoubtedly, the most famous murder in Suffolk history was that of Maria Marten by her lover William Corder in 1828. Known as the 'Murder in the Red Barn' it caused a sensation at the time and for generations afterwards. Until the Jack the Ripper murders in Whitechapel some sixty years later, the story of Maria Martin was the most notorious homicide case of the nineteenth century. Providing the inspiration for everything from sermons to popular plays, numerous features of the case struck a resonance with the mindset of an age which was as sentimental as it was moralistic and judgmental in attitude. With its principal elements of a 'fallen' woman, a ruthless villain, and a sensitive and grieving mother who uncovered the crime against her daughter by psychic means, its appeal was boundless. Indeed, the Red Barn murder and its aftermath were said to embrace almost every aspect of human life, it being a story which encompassed, 'mythology, necromancy, biography, history, theology, phrenology, anatomy, legal ingenuity, conjugal correspondence, amatory epistles, poetry, theatrical representations and affecting anecdotes'. It also generated a classic Bury St Edmunds ghost story and a mystery which is now never likely to be conclusively solved.

The grim tale of the murder has been told many times. The murderer William Corder and his victim Maria Martin were both from the Suffolk village of Polstead but from very different

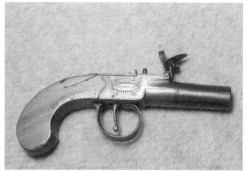

Corder's pistols used in the murder of Maria Marteen and preserved at Moyses Hall Museum. (Stewart Evans)

backgrounds. Corder hailed from a wealthy farming family in the village of Polstead, whilst Maria Martin was a twenty-five-year-old unmarried mother, the daughter of the local mole catcher. Although the pre-Victorian era was far less class conscious than the age which followed, Corder conducted a secret affair with Maria, the result of which was a child who died shortly after birth. It seems that Maria Marten was desirous of Corder marrying her, and on 18 May 1827 it seemed her wish had come true. Corder arrived at the Marten family cottage and announced to her family his intention was to wed Maria. However, it was to be a marriage by licence, with no banns read in church and it was necessary to elope to Ipswich where the ceremony could be conducted. The next day Maria left the cottage to meet Corder at a local landmark known as the Red Barn and was never seen alive again. To avoid suspicion, Corder persuaded her family that Maria was temporarily in lodgings elsewhere, giving the impression that all was well. After a period Corder left the district himself, purportedly to be with Maria, and kept up the pretence she was still alive by means of fictitious communications.

On three successive nights in March 1828, Mrs Marten underwent a recurrent dream in which she saw her daughter murdered and buried in the Red Barn. So convincing was her dream that she persuaded her husband to dig up the floor of the Red Barn on 19 April 1828. First he discovered part of Maria's shawl and 18ins further down part of a human body. Horrified, he ran from the barn and raised the alarm; further excavation by others discovered the remains of Maria which was identified by marks on the teeth and clothing. Suspicions at once fell upon Corder who by this time had moved to London. He had married (via means of a newspaper advertisement to which he received ninety-five replies) and was found to be running a school for young ladies in Ealing, where he was arrested.

Later writers have doubted the story of Mrs Marten's dream, and theorised that she was in some way implicated with the death of her daughter. Certainly, there were doubts expressed at the time and even suggestions that the idea had arisen from a book in the Marten's cottage, *The Old English Baron,* in which a father discovered the body of his daughter as a result of the dream of his wife. Others have seen it as a striking coincidence, the working of intuition or proof of psychic revelation.

Following a medical examination of the body, Corder stood accused of killing Maria by a combination of shooting, stabbing and burial alive in the Red Barn and was committed to Bury St Edmunds Gaol, to await trial. Considered a model prison in its time (even the Czar of Russia sought details regarding it), it contained both female and male prisoners and everyone from serious criminals to debtors whose only failing had been poverty.

In a speed which is admirable compared with today's cumbersome and lengthy criminal process, Corder's trial was set to begin on 7 August 1828. The case came before Lord Chief Baron Alexander but the course of justice was delayed by a near riot by a mob of spectators eager to sit and observe the trial. A near riot occurred as curiosity seekers, many of whom had endured queuing in heavy rain, struggled to gain access. Disorder held up the empanelling of a jury for nearly an hour. Eventually the trial began and witnesses gave evidence for the prosecution.

In contrast with a murder trial today, Corder was deemed incapable of testifying on his own behalf (being considered an interested party under rules of evidence in force until 1898). However, the practice of letting an accused make an unsworn statement from the dock was permitted. For his part, Corder took the opportunity and read from a manuscript his version of the events leading to the death of Maria Marten. It was an unconvincing story and performance, Corder in essence claiming that Maria Marten had committed suicide in the Red Barn following a quarrel. He had panicked and hidden her body, fearing that suspicion would fall upon him. The jury were not impressed and duly returned a verdict of guilty and Corder was sentenced to death. Before he died prison governor Orridge urged Corder to confess his guilt. Corder duly wrote and signed a confession admitting his responsibility for the death of Maria.

On the morning of the execution a crowd of over 1,000 people had gathered by 9 a.m.; by midday the gathering had swollen to an estimated 7,000 (the population of Bury at the time was around 10,000). Workers in Bury were reputed to have gone on strike in order to be present, whilst country people came in on foot for up to twenty miles around to watch the spectacle. It was a long drawn-out affair, with Corder first having an opportunity to visit the chapel and then bid farewell to fellow inmates. A special door was cut in the prison wall to allow egress to the specially constructed gallows erected outside the south wall of the prison (this door was thereafter known in prison slang as 'Corder's eternal way'). He was observed to be resigned to his fate but 'sighing heavily at intervals' and saying in low tones, 'May God forgive me! Lord receive my soul!'. Mounting the scaffold, Corder's last words in a quiet voice were, 'I deserve my fate; I have offended against my God: may He have mercy on my soul.' The confession was readily accepted although during the 1970s a Bury St Edmunds man named Sheen tried to start a campaign to clear Corder's name. There has been no serious doubt about Corder's guilt amongst most analysts of the crime.

During the execution there was some objection vocally directed at the hangman, an executioner named Foxton. Criticisms were directed to the standard of his workmanship, this being the period when the hangman would be responsible for supplying the rope (the identity of these self-appointed experts in the crowd is unknown). Complaints were principally concerned at the quality of the knot and the length of the drop, rather than the fact that when Corder was pushed from the platform, Foxton had to hold the prisoner around the waist and pull, in order to accelerate death. Foxton, who served as hangman at the Old Bailey, was reported to have been personally quite offended by these criticisms. From the closely observed motions of the body, it was estimated that it took about eight minutes for all signs of life to be completely extinguished.

Since the reign of King Henry VIII a small number of the bodies of executed criminals were made available to doctors for dissection. To generations who sincerely believed in the literal resurrection of the body on the Day of Judgement, the prospect of being cut up by anatomists could seem a worse fate than death. Thus, after being left hanging for the customary hour, Corder's body was removed from the gallows and taken to the court at Shire Hall and placed for viewing by the public. It seems the intense interest of the public had not been dispersed by the execution, and crowds again gathered to gape at the body before dissection. It was recorded that, 'many thousands of persons, and some of high respectability, and of both sexes availed themselves of this last opportunity of seeing the remains of him who had so long been the principal theme'. Observers noted the presence of a great many women among those who flocked to view the body.

Artists swiftly arrived to create a death mask (still on view at Moyses Hall Museum in Bury St Edmunds) and experts in the psuedo-science of phrenology pronounced upon the shape of Corder's cranium, finding, 'secretiveness, acquisitiveness, philoprogenitiveness and imitativeness'. Finally, in a touch of horror worthy of Mary Shelley's *Frankenstein*, it was reported that a galvanic battery had been brought over from Cambridge, in order to conduct electrical experiments on the lifeless body.

With justice done, the commercial exploitation of the crime began immediately. Accounts of the trial were soon on sale, with the bookshop selling out of its 500 copies within a few hours. The hangman's rope was cut into pieces and sold off at the price of a guinea an inch to enthusiastic souvenir hunters, whilst Foxton the hangman kept the trousers and socks, 'as of right'. Even ornamental china figures of Maria and William were later manufactured.

Above left: *Corder in a contemporary portrait.*

Above right: *Robert Thurston Hopkins (1884-1958) whose predilection for haunted skulls began with the story of Corder's skull.*

Thus, the Red Barn case entered the small number of English murders which remain in the collective public consciousness for years afterwards. The popular obsession with the events placed Polstead firmly on the tourist trail for as long as key monuments connected with the personalities survived. A public subscription was started to build a special memorial tomb over the body of poor Maria Marten, a plan opposed by the Revd Whitmore who stated that the whole business should be allowed to fade from public memory. Although his hopes about the crime being forgotten were never to be realised, he need not have worried about the presence of a vulgar monument. When a memorial stone was finally erected above Maria Marten's grave, it was soon chipped away by souvenir hunters. Similarly, the Red Barn continued to be a tourist attraction until destroyed by fire later in the nineteenth century.

The Ghost in the Theatre

Like television viewers today, the nineteenth-century theatre audience loved true crime reconstructions. The life and death of Maria Marten and William Corder were the stuff of drama, and the supernatural elements of the story were promoted and exaggerated in stage productions from the outset. In one version, *The Red Barn*, performed at Sadler's Wells theatre in August 1842 featured a ghostly Maria Marten haunting Corder in the condemned cell, terrifying him into writing his confession. Amid stage directions such as *Ghost Music* and *Blue Fire, The Spirit of Maria Marten Appears*, the actress playing her ghost declared:

> Canst thou, murderer, hope that sleep – soft, balmy sleep – can e'er be thine? Look upon thy sinless victim, who in life adored thee, now wandering here, unearthly, pale and cold. See! See! From whence her life-blood gushed. William! William! Thy poor Maria pities and forgives thee – thee, her murderer.

However, despite the emphasis of the supernatural elements in the story, not an ounce of superstition seems to have surrounded Corder's relics or any fears that his vengeful spirit might put in an appearance other than upon the stage. Indeed, there seems to have been no published account of any haunting associated with the Corder case outside fictional dramatisations for nearly a century. The first ghost story may have emerged in the 1870s but no account appeared in print until 1946, the year before Corder's skeleton was moved from the West Suffolk Hospital to Moyses Hall Museum. Nonetheless, it is a classic.

The Haunting of Corder's Skull

Claims of a haunting involved with the skeleton appeared in 1946 with the publication of *Adventures with Phantoms*, the first book of ghost stories penned by the prolific country writer, Robert Thurston Hopkins (1884-1958). Although best known as a writer about Sussex life and ancient buildings, Hopkins had been born at Bury St Edmunds and retained a strong affection for the area into his twilight years, continuing to write for local newspapers in Suffolk into the 1940s. In the last ten years of his life he concentrated on writing about ghosts; indeed, in one article he admitted that as his own earthly life span was running to its close, he would soon be learning the answer to the mystery of life after death. His first collection of stories provided an opportunity for forays into his earliest childhood memories and his upbringing at Gyves

House, part of the old Bury St Edmunds Gaol. Hopkins' father had been an official with the Commission of Prisons and had bought Gyves House when the gaol had finally closed in 1877. Of Gyves House, Hopkins wrote:

> It was a rambling building, sombre and shabby, with red tiled roof, and bleary eyed old windows leaning forward from crooked gables. Inside jutting iron lamp holders held smoky oil lamps, and in the passages, I can still see the flames playing shadow bo-peep with the sombre oil paintings and cases of stuffed owls and other wild birds.

From this loving description of his family home, Hopkins went on to claim that upon the wall was exhibited the last confession of William Corder, not a copy but the actual letter which had been written on the eve of the execution some sixty years before. But this was as nothing to the ghost story told by his father to the family at Christmas time which concerned other relics from the case. The first story in his book, Hopkins claimed he repeated the story in print for the first time, 'without embellishment'.

Following the execution and dissection of Corder's body, a former surgeon at Bury Gaol had tanned the skin and pickled the scalp. In due course the surgeon bequeathed these to a Bury St Edmunds doctor in his will whilst the skeleton went to the West Suffolk Hospital. A Dr Kilner is supposed to have come into possession of the skin and the scalp about 1870 (the latter being presumed to be the one preserved today in Moyses Hall Museum in Bury St Edmunds).

Having inherited these relics, it appears that Dr Kilner was inspired to add Corder's skull to his collection. To this end he resolved to secretly remove it from the skeleton, by then preserved in the museum of the hospital. As the common law stood at the time, a corpse was deemed nobody's property and thus incapable of being stolen. Therefore Dr Kilner would have enjoyed a technical defence to any allegation of theft which might have been raised, but it seems that he wanted to avoid scrutiny and elected to remove the skull by stealth, at night when the museum was empty. Late one evening he entered the exhibition room and lit three candles for illumination. However, his nerve was to be challenged by the strange behaviour of the candles. As soon as all three were lit, one was mysteriously snuffed out. As he turned to relight it, the other two candles went out. Throughout his task Dr Kilner persistently suffered the candle flames being extinguished but managed to keep one alight until he completed his work. He was also later supposed to have admitted that from the first moment he removed the skull he felt very uncomfortable.

Returning home he placed the skull in a cabinet in the drawing room. One evening a few days later a maid came in saying that a gentleman in a top hat and old fashioned clothes had arrived and wished to see him. Dr Kilner went to meet him in the twilight, calling on the servant to bring an oil lantern. On entering the surgery, Dr Kilner thought he glimpsed a figure in the gloom, close to the window, but when the light was brought seconds later the room was found to be empty. Dr Kilner remonstrated with the maid but she insisted that there had been a caller who must have thought better of a consultation and departed.

Dr Kilner soon forgot about the incident. But a few days later he glimpsed a male figure lurking by a summerhouse on the lawn. When he stepped into the garden the form had vanished. Strange phenomena also began to occur inside his house, including the mysterious opening of doors and the sounds of footsteps, heavy breathing and muttering. Members of the household were also disturbed by hammering noises and sobbing emanating from the drawing room in which the skull was kept. More intimately, he was beset by a feeling of unease which robbed him of sleep, and then by bad dreams when he did finally obtain the release of slumber.

Despite his scepticism, Dr Kilner began to link the events with his possession of the skull. He began to think of ways of disposing of it.

The following night he decided to keep his bedroom door open to see if anything would materialise once he had retired to bed. He soon fell asleep, but awoke a few hours later to sounds from downstairs. He lay in bed listening and then, as the noises continued, he went out on to the landing with a candle. In the faint light he looked down the stairs to the drawing room door where he saw a white hand reaching over the glass door knob. The door opened and he heard what sounded like an intruder moving around downstairs.

Overcome by anger rather than fear, Dr Kilner rushed downstairs, armed only with a solid candlestick in one hand as a weapon and the burning candle in the other. In the drawing room he found the box in which the skull was kept had burst into splintered pieces. The cabinet door was open and the skull stood on a shelf inside undamaged and 'grinning malevolently.'

Dr Kilner's determination to rid himself of the skull was now total. He met up with Hopkins' father in Bury St Edmunds and presented him with the skull, allegedly declaring, 'As you are the owner of Corder's condemned cell and the gallows on which he was hanged, perhaps it won't hurt you to take care of his skull!' Hopkins senior willingly accepted custody of the skull, wrapped in a handkerchief, but despite Dr Kilner's hopes, injury very soon followed in its wake. Later that evening, as Hopkins walked down the steps of the Angel Hotel in Bury St Edmunds he stumbled and badly twisted his foot and did not recover for a week. The next day his best horse was fatally injured falling in a chalk pit and over the following weeks he knew, 'illness, sorrow and financial disaster.'

Ascribing these to the influence of the skull, Hopkins' father apparently bribed a gravedigger of a nearby country churchyard to get rid of the relic once and for all. The skull was duly placed in a cash box and committed to the earth in secret. Thereafter, his ill fortune ended.

For his part, Hopkins twice averred that the story was not fiction and that, 'Names, places and dates are openly and correctly stated, and can be verified'. Although writing some seventy years after the alleged events he must have known corroboration would have been difficult to obtain. It must be admitted that Hopkins was keen on stories of haunted skulls, notably those concerning one of the screaming skulls of Warbleton Priory, Sussex, which was exposed in the lanes of Brighton and associated with order manifestations over many years (see the book *Haunted Brighton* published by Tempus). It could be that Hopkins' fascination for skulls was initially sparked in his childhood by the story of the Corder relic. Although not as famous as many other legendary screaming skulls, the Hopkins story contains motifs and details which occur in other such tales as well as those involving 'cursed' Egyptian relics which enjoyed particular vogue in the 1920s and 1930s, following the discovery of Tutankhamen's tomb in 1922. The alleged manifestations experienced in the Kilner resemble those linked with the claimed haunting of the lid of a mummy case in the British Museum (also cited by Thurston Hopkins in his book *Ghosts Over England*, 1953) and disturbances at the home of Sir Alexander Seton in Edinburgh in 1936, attributed to a cursed bone taken from a tomb near the Pyramids.

In 1947 the hospital authorities decided to part with their famous specimen. Whether this was motivated by the publication of Hopkins' story or a reforming zeal to do away with all relics of the past with the newly established National Health Service is not known, but the skeleton was passed to Moyses Hall Museum. Eventually, it was transferred to the Royal Hunterian Museum, maintained by the Royal College of Surgeons in Lincoln's Inn, London, where it stayed until 2004. Regrettably, in that year the museum gave in to demands to destroy the skeleton which emanated from a woman named Miss Nessworthy who claimed a relation to the Corder family, via her grandmother. In what many saw as a capitulation to misplaced notions of political correctness, the museum duly surrendered the bones which were then swiftly burnt at a crematorium. The original order of the Assize Court and the interests of future generations, curious about the historic interaction between medicine and the law, did not seem to come into consideration.

Miss Nessworthy seems to have gained some kind of personal triumph from this outcome and fears were expressed that the book bound in Corder's skin and his scalp at Moyses Hall Museum might similarly be removed and destroyed to her satisfaction as well. Fortunately, no legal precedent was set by the action of destroying the bones and the curators of Moyses Hall in Bury St Edmunds appear to be made of sterner stuff than the Royal Hunterian Museum. Obviously, as regards the ghost story, modern DNA testing techniques could have settled the provenance of the skull once and for all, using a sample from either the scalp or the skin-bound book as a comparison. Even if the tale of Dr Kilner's substitution of the skull is fiction, it is easy to envisage that the original might have been replaced with another anatomical specimen during display and use over a period of more than 100 years. Until recent amendments of the Anatomy Act 1834, the treatment of hospital specimens could be a very casual affair. Indeed, it is known that during the 1940s trainee nurses and doctors at Bury St Edmunds would take the Corder skeleton to hospital dances (how the hours must have flown by). It is easy to see the scope for mishaps and damage which might lead to a replacement being needed. Sadly, as ashes tell no tales, the matter now cannot be settled by forensic tests, but a suspicion must remain that the wrong skull went up in smoke in 2004.

For his part, Thurston Hopkins offered the following admonished, '… if ever you come across a tortoiseshell tinted skull in a japanned cash box leave it severely alone. If you take it home there will be the Devil to Pay – and you may not be prepared to meet his bill'. He repeated the warning seven years later in *Ghosts over England* (1953).

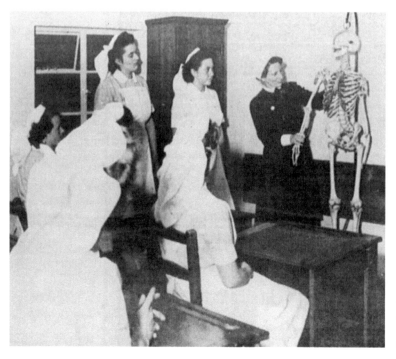

Corder's skeleton being used as an anatomical specimen in the 1940s. Was the skull the original?

The Haunting of Gyves House

In his later account of the haunting of Corder's skull published in 1953, Hopkins makes the claim that Gyves House was haunted:

> ... invisible presences were always with one and whispered in haunting undertones. Mysterious knockings and ghosts were all around in the stone-ribbed prison buildings, occurring both day and night. We became so accustomed to them that we ceased to feel any fear.

Unfortunately, Hopkins gives nothing away beyond these tantalising remarks.

However, a later occupant of Gyves House stated that she had seen a male apparition in old fashioned clothing inside her house, during the 1980s and 1990s. She identified this as William Corder, although given the large number of male prisoners who worked or were incarcerated at the jail in its history, this identification might be in some doubt. Nonetheless, she was convinced that it was none other than Corder returning to the site where thousands had flocked in 1828 to witness his death.

It is also of interest to note that stories of a haunting have circulated in Polstead since the 1960s. These received national publicity after a newly installed rector and his family fled Polstead Rectory in July 1978 only a few days after having taken up residence. The widow of a former rector confirmed that strange sounds had been heard in the rectory in the past, although a group of investigators and journalists from the East Anglian Psychical Research Unit encountered nothing in an overnight vigil. Soon after, the Church of England sold the rectory off to a private buyer who refused to discuss the matter thereafter. Several investigators speculated whether the events might be linked with the Red Barn murder and a local tradition averred that even the Revd Whitmore had returned in spectral form, driving a coach and horses down a hill.

The Nichols Murder

Less well known, but in some ways more shocking for its casual brutality, is the story of what became known as the Nichols murder, the victim and perpetrators coming from the same family. It occurred near the small village of Fakenham Magna, north of Bury St Edmunds, in 1793 and is another crime that illustrates the impact a murder can have on local memory and leave a legacy of macabre and ghostly stories. Over 100 years later, well into the twentieth century, the Breckland naturalist W.G. Clarke recorded in his classic work *In Breckland Wilds* (1925), 'Even this quiet village has been the scene of a tragedy, of which the people of the district still talk with bated breath.' The event which had so lingered in folk memory was the brutal killing of seventeen-year-old Sarah Nichols, slain by her own father and brother. John Nichols was a carpenter (though in later folk versions he was elevated to a farmer).

On the evening of 14 September 1793, Sarah Nichols was sent out from her cottage on an errand from her mother, to buy 3st of flour from the Fox Inn at Honington. She never returned and the next morning her body was found lying in a ditch, a cord around the neck, by Mr Pendle from the Fox Inn. He rushed to inform the Nichols family of the killing of their daughter and on arrival at the cottage was shaken by the chilling detachment of the family to the news. No-one in the family seemed particularly moved on learning Sarah had been found dead; her mother continued making dumplings and seemed more concerned about not disturbing her husband. On learning of his daughter's death, John Nichols remarked, 'Dear Lord, have mercy upon me' eight times in what seems to have been a contrived appearance of grief. His son Nathan said nothing at all and both men went out together shortly afterwards.

Of course, it might be said that the Nichols family were dealing with grief in their own personal way, but the community were in no doubt that guilt for the crime lay within the family. The body of Sarah was collected on a hurdle and an inquest was conducted soon afterwards. The initial proceedings seem to have been rather confused with several adjournments, but it may well have been here that village gossip surfaced and the evidence was considered sufficient to charge John and Nathan jointly with murder. Father and son were taken into custody, and once inside Ipswich Gaol Nathan readily confessed to having killed his sister at the instigation of his father.

It was Nathan's damning confession which was later read out before the Assize Court, at the trial of father and son in Bury St Edmunds the following March. In his confession Nathan admitted he had been out with his father who had plucked a hedge stake from a fence and commanded him to knock his sister down with it. Too frightened to disobey his father, Nathan duly struck Sarah repeatedly with the stake, with fatal results. John Nichols then ordered his son to tie one of her garters around her neck, to make it appear the cause of death had been strangulation and they cast her body into a ditch and returned home.

As well as the confession, neighbours gave evidence of Sarah being ill-treated by all her family, whilst Sarah's sister Elizabeth gave evidence that her father and brother had both been out on the night in question and had returned together. The judge, Sir William Henry Ashurst, directed the jury that the confession might not be considered sufficient evidence on its own, but taken with other circumstantial evidence, a charge of murder might be sustained. The jury quickly returned a verdict of guilty against both men and the judge sentenced both to death, the sentence to be carried out within forty-eight hours. The judge remarked that John Nichols was guilty of a monstrous depravity in instigating one of his children to murder another, quite exceeding anything in his judicial experience.

The next day Nathan recanted his confession, saying that he had only admitted to killing his sister on the advice of a prisoner in Ipswich Gaol the previous year, in the hope of receiving a lenient sentence. However, following further questioning, he soon capitulated and admitted this recantation was a falsehood inspired by John Nichols, explaining that he had only tried to withdraw his confession under pressure from his father to do so, once again revealing the malign power which John wielded over his son. Once again Nathan admitted the crime saying that Sarah was not dead when he had finished beating her but was dead when he returned to hide her body. He hinted that his step-mother was implicated in the crime. He stated that a week before, his stepmother had spoken to his father and said he, 'must do something with the girl, for she could do nothing with her' but was unaware of a plan to murder her until his father had ordered him to kill her. On the Monday following the murder he heard his step-mother scalding Elizabeth, the youngest daughter, and saying, 'She wished they (John and Nathan) had killed her too'.

However, these revelations were to have no bearing on Nathan's guilt or the sentence he faced. Since a Court of Criminal Appeal would not exist for over a century, there was no mechanism whereby any part of the proceedings could have been challenged (save other than by the intervention of the King). Even if an appeal by Nathan had been possible, a defence of duress has never been available as a defence to murder in English law.

Father and son were hanged on 26 March 1794, just outside the Northgate in Bury St Edmunds, almost certainly upon Thingoe Hill, which had been used as an execution site since the seventeenth century (forty alleged witches had been hanged there in 1644). Both men

THE

T R I A L

OF

JOHN and NATHAN NICHOLS,

(FATHER and SON)

FOR THE MURDER OF

SARAH NICHOLS,

Daughter of JOHN, and Sister of NATHAN.

LIST OF THE JURY.

JAMES RAYNHAM, Brettenham	JOHN ENNALLS, Hitcham
JOHN WICKS, Newmarket	THOMAS KEMBALL, ditto
JOHN WARNER, ditto	JOHN BENNETT, ditto
ROBERT BRIDGEMAN, ditto	ROBERT LUCKEY, ditto
WILLIAM ROSE, Brettenham	JOHN GOTTS, Hawkedon
JOHN RANSON, Hitcham	JAMES SIMPSON, Shimpling

JOHN and NATHAN NICHOLS *(Father and Son)* were *indicted, for having, on the 14th of September, maliciously and wickedly murdered* Sarah Nichols, *Daughter of the said* John, *and Sister of the said* Nathan Nichols, *by cruelly beating and afterwards strangling the said* Sarah Nichols, *so as to occasion her death, in the Parish of* Fakenham, *in the County of Suffolk.*

MR. SELLON, as junior Counsel, opened the Prosecution, and stated the general tenour of the indictment.

Mr. Serjeant LE BLANC then addressed the Jury; he observed, that from the multiplicity of evidence necessary to adduce, he should be compelled to trespass on their patience; but when they had heard the different testimonies; when they had maturely considered the nature of the offence they were about to try; when they had reflected on the enormity of it, aggravated as it was by the affinity or relationship which the Prisoners bore to the deceased, he trusted they would patiently wait, attentively listen, and not think their time ill bestowed. He then proceeded to state the evidence he meant to bring forward in support of the charge.

The frontispiece of a contemporary account of the trial of John and Nathan Nichols, 1794.

asserted their innocence again on the gallows, the *Norwich Post* newspaper report recording that, 'the behaviour of the elder Nichols was very undaunted, as he gave away his hat and neck cloth to some persons standing in the crowd with apparent unconcern.' Ascending the ladder he told spectators, 'Life is but a short passage, and now I am at the last step; of the crime for which I am going to suffer I am entirely innocent.'

Following execution, the body of Nathan Nichols was sent for dissection, whilst that of his father was taken for gibbeting at the scene of the crime. The *Bury and Norwich Post* reported that several thousand people went to Fakenham Magna in the next few weeks to see the body. Even allowing for exaggeration, this would suggest it was a popular attraction despite the remoteness of the spot. Placed inside an iron cage and exposed to the elements, the decaying body of John Nichols remained a gruesome warning to passing travellers and residents for a number of years. Although intended to promote respect for the law, its presence was probably not conducive to local mental health or welfare.

The Fakenham Ghost

Not surprisingly, the area around the specially constructed gibbet was considered an uncanny spot to be avoided at night. One night, around 1800, an elderly woman walking in terror of ghosts and goblins had her worst fears realised when she heard pattering footsteps behind her.

The gibbeted body of John Nichols was a macabre spectacle for years in the neighbourhood.

Her fear increased as she tried her best to flee and the footsteps followed. Looking round she saw a menacing shape in the darkness which sent her into a blind panic. Eventually she reached the door of her daughter's cottage and fainted on the step. Her husband and daughter opened the door to find both the lady and recognise the cause of her terror standing behind her in the darkness. The apparition turned out to be a young donkey foal which had lost its mother. The occurrence was celebrated in a poem *The Fakenham Ghost* by farm labourer turned poet, Robert Bloomfield (1766-1823):

> The Candle's gleam pierc'd through the night,
> Some short space o'er the green;
> And there the little trotting Sprite
> Distinctly might be seen
>
> An Ass's foal had lost its Dam
> Within the spacious park;
> And simple as the playful lamb,
> Had follow'd in the dark.

The Fakenham Ghost which terrified an old woman but turned out to be a young donkey.

THE FAKENHAM GHOST.

The story caused much amusement locally and the family subsequently adopted the animal and raised it as a pet.

In another story, some years after the execution, a group of locals gathered at the Fox public house at Honington and conversation turned to the crime. One man laid a bet with another that he dared not go to the gibbet and ask the decaying corpse how he felt. The wager was accepted and the intrepid man set off on a lonely walk across the fields. To the sound of the creaking of the gibbet timbers and the rattling of the chains, the grisly spectacle of Nichols' body loomed above in him the darkness. Summoning his courage he addressed the mangled body, 'Well, Naabour Nichols, how do you fale?' and was horrified to hear a gruff voice replying, 'Wet, cold and hungry, and tired of being here!' The man who had laid the bet had taken a short cut across the fields, arriving ahead of his friend to scare him. Variants of the story have the victim of the prank running all the way to Ixworth or dying of shock on the spot. The story is an old rural example of what we today class as an urban myth, a popular tale told in many places and by no means exclusive to the area.

The gibbet remained a spectacle for a number of years, until the structure eventually fell down. Local lore attributed various destinations for parts of the structure. The iron cage and what remained of Nichols were then buried. According to folklore, parts of the gibbet were buried in a clay pit at Willow Hall whilst other parts were put to practical use to provide a bridge over a dyke at Honington.

A reminder of the case came in 1936 during excavations for Honington Aerodrome when what remained of the gibbet cage and the skeleton of John Nichols were unearthed. The soles of his shoes were still intact and teeth remained in the skull, although they fell out within forty-eight hours. A group of archaeologists excavating a Roman villa at Stanton Chair arrived and examined the bones and amazed the building contractors by sitting and eating their lunch around the skeleton which was later reburied nearby, though the workmen preferred to stay well clear of it. The gibbet cage was later displayed in Moyses Hall Museum in Bury St Edmunds.

Into the 1980s a story persisted, claiming that there was a spot on the RAF base at Honington which was haunted, with guard dogs reacting to the atmosphere and barking furiously. This was considered to be the spot where the gibbet cage had been found.

FOUR

GHOSTS AROUND
THE TOWN

The Angel Hotel

Built upon land that has been the site of an inn since the fifteenth century, the Angel Hotel has been the premier hotel in Bury St Edmunds since the Regency era. Standing opposite the Abbey Gateway, this fine example of a Georgian building has recently lost one charming feature from its exterior. This was a wonderful covering of virginia creeper which had grown completely across the frontage over the space of many years, removed at the order of the authorities who claimed it was necessary on grounds of health and safety.

One wonders how such bureaucratic canard would have been viewed by one of the Angel's most celebrated guests, Charles Dickens. The Angel was well known to Dickens – who was a great lover of ghost stories – and he immortalised the Angel in *Pickwick Papers*. He later stayed at the Angel when lecturing at the nearby Athenaeum Assembly Hall (see Athenaeum Lane). Less impressed with the hotel was the Edwardian ghost story collector and authority on old inns, Charles G. Harper, who described the Angel as, 'a dyspeptic and gloomy looking house of huge proportions and sad coloured brick.'

Not surprisingly, the Angel has celebrated Dickens's judgment and ignored Harper's criticism. The Angel still contains the Pickwick Bar and the Dickens Room, a luxury bedroom, commemorating its illustrious literary association and also said to be haunted. A journalist from a woman's magazine who stayed at the Angel during the late 1970s made a point of staying in the Dickens Room in the hope of encountering the ghost. She slept soundly, apart from hearing a series of banging sounds at one point, the cause of which was not discovered. There might well have been a normal explanation for these, perhaps noises echoing up from some other part of the large hotel. Other stories tell of the strange disappearance of objects belonging to staff in the Dickens Room but again it is easy to postulate a normal explanation.

The Angel Hotel incorporates medieval stone cellars which are now used as a dining room and it would be easy to imagine that they were connected with the nearby Abbey. One story asserts that there is a tunnel which runs under the Angel Hill to the One Bull pub in Eastgate Street;

Above: *The Angel Hotel.*

Left: *Athenaeum Lane, allegedly haunted by a ghostly young woman.*

a bricked up entrance in the cellar was put forward in folk tradition as the entrance to the tunnel in which a fiddler once vanished. The story – which is known at many locations throughout the British Isles – avers that when the tunnel was rediscovered nobody dared enter it. However, a fiddler rashly volunteered to explore it, accompanied by his dog. He said he would play his violin so that people could trace his course by listening to the music above the ground. People followed the music but at a certain point upon the Angel Hill it ceased and the fiddler was never seen again; in another version only the fiddler's terrified dog emerged from the tunnel. Nobody dared enter the tunnel to mount a rescue and it was sealed up. The Bury St Edmunds legend may be one of the oldest documented recorded examples of the tradition, for it appears in Richard Yates' *History* of Bury St Edmunds, first published in 1820.

On various occasions psychics and mediums visiting the Angel have claimed that there are at least two haunting entities in the hotel. Like all too many such claims they are incapable of independent verification and corroboration but, interestingly, they have all tended to identify the cellar as the site of the haunting which may be suggestive of a presence.

Athenaeum Lane

Major writers such as Charles Dickens and William Thackeray lectured at the Athenaeum building in its heyday, and the Astronomer Royal established a large telescope in the roof. No stories are associated with the Athenaeum building itself, but the narrow pedestrian lane which runs alongside it is held in local lore to be haunted by the phantom of a woman. One story collected by the former curator of the Manor House Museum, Alan Scott-Davis, is that the ghost is a woman who fled from the Widow's Coffee House near the Norman Tower which was

– at least according to what are almost certainly spurious local traditions – a front for a house of ill-repute. However, as she made her escape she was knocked down by a passing carriage.

According to Alan Scott-Davis and H. Greengrass who included the story in a short guidebook *Ghosts of Bury St Edmunds* in 2000, the apparition is said to make its way into Abbeygate Street where the phantom lady is said to take to the air. It is possible that this story may be a garbled variant of the legend of the Grey Lady discussed in Chapter two.

Bridewell Lane

Two premises in Bridewell Lane had a reputation for being haunted during the 1970s. One was the Blackbirds Pub which shut down early in the decade and stood empty for a period. Nonetheless, whilst unoccupied, neighbours told police that they heard noises emanating from the building in the early hours which suggested that it was still in use as a pub. The clink of glasses was heard and there were muffled sounds of voices, as though a drinks party was going on. The cause of these noises was never ascertained; perhaps in some spectral form the pub was replaying the sounds of happy times.

A second site in the street is the former Marlows Timber merchants building (the firm having since relocated to the outskirts of Bury St Edmunds). This was the scene of poltergeist phenomena in the summer of 1976. Planks of wood were reportedly seen rising in the air by terrified staff. The disturbances seemed to focus around an eighteen-year-old employee, typical of the pattern of many poltergeist phenomena which often involve teenagers. Like so many others, the Marlows poltergeist was short-lived, much to the relief of the staff, though occasionally such mysterious incidents seem fixed upon a place rather than a particular individual.

The Clock Museum, Angel Hill (now closed)

In 1951 Frederic Gershom-Parkington (1886-1952) bequeathed a magnificent collection of clocks and time pieces to the people of Bury St Edmunds under the terms of his will. The gift was in memory of his son John who had died in action in the Second World War. For many years these were housed in a museum in a corner of the Angel Hill, close to the borough offices. One of the most important collections of timepieces in the UK, it also housed a number of paintings forming part of the St Edmundsbury Borough Collection. These collections were then moved to the Manor House Museum in 1987 and remained on display until the spring of 2006 when the local authority put into effect a sudden decision to close it.

Amongst the paintings is a portrait which became associated with a haunting of the old clock museum. The ghost is said to be that of Lady Penelope Hervey, her portrait painted by the celebrated Bury artist Mary Beale around 1660. Penelope Hervey inherited the Hengrave estate following the death of her mother and was immediately approached by fortune hunting suitors. Three titled suitors made their intention of being married abundantly clear – Sir George Trenchard, Sir John Gage and Sir William Hervey. Lady Penelope is reputed to have accepted all three proposals, with the proviso that she would marry them each in turn. The first marriage to Sir George in 1610 ended in unknown circumstances two years later and the second to Sir John Gage endured for thirty years, until his death, whereupon she married William Hervey.

The portrait preserved at the Clock Museum showed her in widow's mourning dress and seemed able to generate spooky feelings in those viewing it. In July 1987, art historian Chris

Reeve told the *Bury Free Press*, 'She has the sort of eyes which follow you around. I used to sleep here and when I came in late at night I could feel her eyes on the back of my neck. It's thought she might haunt the staircase. When you look at her she looks incredibly sinister, especially after dark.' Later in 1987 the collection of clocks and paintings were transferred to the Manor House Museum and at the time of writing their fate is uncertain (see below).

In light of this, it would not be surprising if the ghost of Frederic Gershom Partington himself begins to walk. Not only did the local authority plans draw up a scheme to disperse his collection of clocks and use the money from the trust for its own ends, but in August 2006 the council branded his grave as unsafe and were trying to trace any living relatives on whom they could serve a bill, rather than cover the cost of repairs themselves.

The Constitutional Club, Guildhall Street

The Constitutional Club has stood in Guildhall Street since 1888 and was the scene of unexplained incidents just over a century after its foundation. Early on the morning of Sunday 23 April 1989, the club steward Mr Martin Eke, who lived in a flat with his family in the building, heard the sound of people coming up the staircase. Both his wife and son were woken by the noises, although his young daughter slept through it. He got up to find his twelve-year-old son Matthew at the front of the self-contained flat. He had heard someone knock at the door and heard a woman's voice asking to be let in. Looking through the keyhole he had seen nothing.

Thinking burglars were on premises, Mr Eke called the police who arrived very quickly. Despite a thorough search of all areas nothing was discovered. There was no sign of a forced entry or even a forced exit as might have occurred had someone been trapped inside the building. Mr Eke told the local press, 'It was scary. I have no explanation and neither did the police. It sounded like a group of people and yet Matthew heard a woman's voice. I don't particularly believe in ghosts, but I don't have any other explanation.'

Mr Eke also recalled a strange incident where fire doors mysteriously opened by themselves. For their part the club owners remained baffled as to the causes. Although having just celebrated its 100th anniversary, there was no previous record of a haunting at the club, though it is interesting to note that the phenomena happened not long after Mr Eke and his family had moved in. Manifestations shortly after the arrival of a new occupier is a pattern which has been noted with haunted pubs (see Cupola House). The incident lived on in the collective memory of the police in Bury St Edmunds for many years and was never solved.

Railway Station, Fornham Road

Mysterious sounds are not confined to buildings in the town centre. Situated along Fornham Road and Out Northgate, is Bury St Edmunds' railway station which has also been haunted by mysterious footsteps in recent years. The railway first came to Bury St Edmunds in the mid-nineteenth century and the current station, which dates from 1874, was originally one of two which served the town, the other in Eastgate Street. At one time the Fornham Road station employed over 250 staff, the railway being a major hub in the once-extensive East Anglian rail network.

Footsteps and other noises were heard late into the night on Platform 2 of the station, serving passengers for trains to Ipswich and Harwich. Between 2002 and 2004 the office of a transport development company was situated on Platform 2, and was often occupied late in the evening.

Described as heavy and slow, the footsteps would be heard coming along the platform and past the door of the office and then ceasing. Staff from the office would immediately go out on the platform, only to find it completely deserted. Failing to find any cause for the noises, the staff attributed the footsteps to an unknown ghost. Sounds were also heard emanating from unoccupied rooms beneath Platform 2 which at one time housed a dance studio, but these might have been attributable to the vibration of nearby traffic or the settling of the building.

Since the footsteps were heard, parts of the Bury station have been substantially refurbished and the offices all moved to the ground floor. According to staff now working at the station this seems to have brought an end to the phenomena, with the identity of the haunting presence remaining a mystery.

The Grapes Public House

The Grapes stands at the top of St Andrew's Street (north) and the corner of Brentgovel Street. A popular town centre pub much frequented by local customers, it was once a small coaching inn. In recent years it has acquired a reputation for being haunted by an invisible ghost. Although locals have stories, the current licensees – who have much experience in the liquor trade – have not experienced anything and prefer to take the view that the Grapes is not haunted. However, since October 2005, Stephen Chaplin, who undertakes cleaning and maintenance duties at the pub, has had a number of unusual experiences. Initially, he ascribed these to the effects of suggestion and the empty silence of the deserted pub early in the morning when the only occasional sound has been the calls of pigeons on the roof. However, repeated odd incidents have persuaded him otherwise, including a strong sense of a presence coming up behind him and seeing dark, single figures, 'like sharply defined shadows'. Other incidents have included the unexplained slamming of doors and a sudden feeling of cold, even when the heating is full on. These experiences have occurred in the function room, the bar and the enclosed courtyard of the pub. In his response to the incidents, Stephen is refreshingly philosophical, explaining his attitude as, 'They're obviously not harmful, let's just get on with it.'

Local belief ascribes the haunting to the ghost of a previous landlord who died accidentally from a fall in the cellar, 'during an argument with his wife'. Never having succeeded in putting his view across, his brooding ghost is put forward as the prime candidate as the entity responsible for the manifestations.

The Manor House

Perhaps it was a degree of personal pride that led Alan Scott-Davies, a former manager of the now-closed Manor House Museum, to declare, 'the Manor House Museum must come tops when it comes to haunting' in 2000. He went so far as to state that there were a, 'staggering eleven ghosts, including a family no less.'

In 1961 a correspondent named Elton Halliley wrote to the *Bury Free Press* with a story about the building. Elton Halliley had been the political agent to Walter Guinness, the local MP, who lived in the Manor House. One night Raymond Green, a close friend, spent the night there, but complained that he had experienced a dreadful night. He was convinced that it was haunted by a monk, and he said he would never sleep there again. Elton Halliley said that Walter Guinness had heard other rumours that this room was haunted, but that after the experience of Raymond Green, who was not easily scared, it was decided to keep the room locked.

Above: *Unexplained footsteps were reported on Platform 2 between 2002–2004.*

Left: *The very haunted Manor House Museum.*

In 1999 more ghosts were reported in the Manor House. Alan Scott-Davies, who had become manager the previous year, said that on the Sunday after Christmas 1998 he was in the old kitchen area when he saw a man come out of one door and walk through another door straight ahead. At first he thought it was a colleague but soon realised there was no way the man could have gone through the door because it is simply a panel which has been plastered over:

> I saw him clearly, he looked very real and I saw the back of his head, he had dark hair and was wearing a long Victorian-style black coat and grey pinstripe trousers. The detail was so vivid but it gave me quite a turn afterwards. We think he might have been a butler because where he went through the panel there used to be steps down to the cellar.

Alan Scott-Davies later confirmed these details showing inquirers the door where it took place, and adding the unreported detail that the ghost had walked straight through a blocked doorway at floor level, although there was a step leading up at the foot of the door.

Other staff members said that they had seen a fuzzy figure suspended from a beam in a garret window, where a chamber maid called Sarah hanged herself a century previously (ironically a room that was being converted into an office for Alan Scott-Davies). Once a member of staff saw a woman in a long dress crossing the museum's small garden, and passing through a wall. Tracing the route on plans, Alan Scott-Davies found there to have been a garden path that was later built over. A figure of a Roundhead was also seen to walk across the courtyard next to the museum tearooms, straight through both courtyard walls before disappearing. Whilst pulling at one door handle he then walks through another door.

Other remarkable phenomena included a chilly atmosphere and cold spots that many visitors had felt in one upstairs room. These could be so unpleasant that some people felt compelled to come back downstairs. Alan Scott-Davis identified this as the only regular bedroom in the house when it was a private residence, used by Lady Bristol for overnight stays. Yet he was unaware of Walter Guinness's experiences with the same room. It was added that the room had felt less cold since an adjoining dressing room had been opened.

At the time of writing, the future of the Manor House is uncertain, following a controversial closure by the local authority. However, such a collection of ghosts is likely to prove difficult to disperse.

Mustow Street/Eastgate Street

In 1984, the East Anglian writer, the late H. Mills West, published an account of a pair of phantoms seen in the Mustow Street/ Eastgate Street area. Appearing in his book *Ghosts of East Anglia*, under the heading, 'Figures from the past', the story was told in the first person, from the perspective of a woman drawing upon her childhood memories. According to the account, the unnamed narrator was one of two young sisters, ten and eleven, who were walking home along Eastgate Street with their mother, one Saturday afternoon in October, early in the twentieth century.

Not far from the railway station which once stood in Eastgate Street, all three were surprised to see a man and a woman crossing the road, in the direction of a thickly overgrown area known locally as the Glen. They noticed that the couple appeared to be very lightly clothed for the season and weather that day, it being a bitterly cold afternoon. The woman was wearing a white uniform like a nurse, whilst the man appeared to be in white undergarments. The couple clung

The Suffolk Hotel, early twentieth century.

to each other, the nurse supporting the man who seemed to be badly injured and on the verge of collapse. The reaction of the girls was curiosity, both being struck how incongruous the pair seemed. In contrast, their mother seemed agitated and most insistent that they should leave the scene as soon as possible.

As dusk was falling they heard a scream from the Glen but again their mother refused to stop and hurried them home.

On arriving home, they related their experience to their grandmother. She told them the figures were ghosts, dating from a tragic love affair during the time of the Crimean War. A nurse named Mary Treese fell in love with a soldier who was recovering from wounds in a local hospital but their relationship was condemned by her obsessive father who feared for his daughter's honour. Armed with a shotgun he sought out his daughter and her lover and fatally wounded the man with a shotgun. The father was later hanged for his crime.

In November 2002 I met Diane McKillon, a Bury St Edmunds lady whose mother had been one of the two girls involved in the sighting. Diane McKillon confirmed the story and was able to correct some of the elements in the printed account, based on her mother's recollections of the incident. She stated that her mother's experience took place about 1935 and that she had been with a childhood friend, not with her sister. The two figures had been seen as described, and the sighting corresponded with a passing car stalling suddenly in the street, and a sensation as though a gust of wind was blowing by them. Shortly afterwards they also heard a sound like a gunshot, as well as a scream as they hastened from the scene.

Traditionally, the pair of fleeing lovers are said to return each 20 October to Eastgate Street, reputedly the anniversary of the shooting.

Suffolk Hotel

Before its closure on Christmas Eve 1996, the Suffolk Hotel on the Buttermarket was the scene of regular manifestations. These were popularly attributed to the Grey Lady, but in fact appear to originate from a much more recent tragedy.

The inn once formed part of property controlled by Bury St Edmunds Abbey and was first known as The Greyhound. It was reputedly established as long ago as the reign of Edward I, for an Abbey house is recorded as standing on the site in 1295. Certainly, its role as an inn by 1539 is established beyond doubt by a document recording it as *le Greyhounde* and rented to a Thomas Brown for £5 6s 8d following the surrender of the Abbey to the Crown. The building was wholly rebuilt in 1833 with the exception of flint-walled cellars and the name changed to the Suffolk Hotel, by which time it functioned as a coaching inn (it was established as a posting inn in 1823).

Norman Withington worked as a night porter at the Suffolk Hotel for over six years until its closure in 1996. He noted a number of strange experiences by staff and guests, as well as encountering phenomena for himself. One particular room at the Suffolk Hotel, known as No. 63 among staff, possessed a reputation for being haunted after being the scene of the suicide by a woman doctor, around 1980.

Whilst working there over the years Norman noticed that from time to time a smell of a woman's perfume pervaded room No. 63. On one occasion he believed that there must be a single female guest but later that night (or early in the morning), the single male occupant returned. Surprised by this, Norman followed the guest to check that he was the only occupant and found that the smell had gone without explanation. On other occasions the smell was experienced when the room was unoccupied. Another member of the staff once entered the room to find it, 'ice cold, like a fridge.' On several occasions Norman experimented by waiting alone in the room in the dark, but he did not experience any manifestations.

One morning Norman spoke to another male guest who indicated he wanted to have a confidential word with him. The man asked if the room he had been staying in was haunted. Not wishing to either scare the guest or damage the hotel's reputation, Norman tactfully replied that there was no information he could give. The man then explained in a confidential tone that he was a businessman who had been staying in room No. 63. The purpose for his visit had been for an adulterous liaison with his female secretary. During the night they were disturbed by rattling sounds which kept coming from the wardrobe. The noises ceased as soon as the light was put on. Getting out of bed and examining the wardrobe the businessman could find no explanation. On returning to the bed, the light was extinguished and the sounds returned again. The effect of this was to make the woman increasingly frightened and hysterical as the sounds started each time the light was put out. Their night of illicit passion well and truly disrupted by the phenomena, they remained with the light on for the rest of the night.

The haunted room's reputation was known beyond the hotel staff and salesmen attached to Nilfisk, a local firm, always refused accommodation in room No. 63 and the two adjoining rooms, and would go to another hotel if these were the only rooms available. The Ghost Club made some enquiries into the events and considered an investigation in 1993, but this did not take place.

About 1 a.m. one morning, Norman was on duty at the reception desk when he looked up after seeing a movement from the corner of his eye. (Psychic activity is traditionally seen from the corner of the eye.) Gliding up the stairs were two grey shadowy figures, making no sound. Astonished by the figures, Norman watched them for a moment, doubting the evidence of his senses. Then, impelled by his sense of duty, Norman rose from his desk to chase them, only to see them fade away. Somewhat shaken he returned to his desk, but he did not report the incident for fear of being accused of drinking at work.

At various times Norman heard strange sounds in the hotel, but he was not worried by all of them, dismissing many as due to ordinary causes. But one puzzling incident was when the sound of whispering voices was heard in the kitchen, where Norman's wife Jenny experienced a female apparition. In the summer of 1995, Jenny called in to see Norman and keep him company for part of the night shift. On entering the hotel kitchen she was shocked to see the semi-transparent figure of a woman in grey gliding towards the back door of the kitchen which was visible through it. The figure disappeared into the door. Norman, who was present, did not see the figure but watched his wife 'going as white as a ghost', the hairs on her arms rising in alarm.

Another phenomenon reported by staff at the Suffolk Hotel was the sound of rattling keys accompanied by the sense of a presence which seemed to move through the building. Like many otherwise anonymous manifestations in Bury, this was ascribed to the ubiquitous Grey Lady but the transformation of the hotel into branches of Ottakers's Bookshop (now Waterstones) and the Edinburgh Woollen Mill seem to have brought manifestations to at least a temporary halt.

The Nutshell

One of the best candidates for the title of 'the smallest pub in England' is the much-loved Nutshell, standing on the corner of the Traverse. The tiny Nutshell has a strong popular following as a local drinking institution, although this enthusiasm has not always been shared by big business or the local authority. Amid the globalised mono-culture that has led to bland streets in so many parts of Britain, the Nutshell stands out as a welcome anomaly, a refreshing change from the dominance of corporate chained coffee houses and hangar-sized pubs, a reminder of a time when even the smallest traders could set up taverns without bureaucratic restrictions and exorbitant business rates killing off their enterprises. The building dates from around 1800, and it is believed to have been a fruiterer's business in the 1820s before becoming a tavern later in the nineteenth century.

In the first half of the twentieth century, the Nutshell was also a microscopic museum, housing a fine display of curios, including ancient weapons, a painting of a moonlit lake with shading enhanced by intricately cut pieces of paper and a remarkable 'sand toy', the figure of an acrobat animated on the principle of an hourglass. For years, these exhibits were garlanded with an impressive collection of dust and cobwebs, it being a tradition recorded in 1946 that, 'not a single item of the collection has ever been dusted since the day it was first introduced.' Alas, such eccentricities are no longer tolerated, but among the strange objects still hanging from the ceiling of the bar are the bones of a human foot and a highly revered mummified cat. The cat is perhaps 200 years older than the Nutshell, originally having been found in the wall of a pub which once stood in St John's Street. It is one of a number of preserved cats which have been discovered in old buildings, and which have strange stories associated with them, the most notable being at Fakenham Magna in 1972 (see Chapter five). Such feline burials seem to have been made as foundation sacrifices during the construction of buildings, and also considered protection against magic or pestilence – the symbolic presence of a cat being imagined as a deterrent against infestation by vermin.

Today the Nutshell cat is regarded with curious but guarded affection – local superstitions still aver that it is bad luck to either remove or even touch it. In September 1982 it was stolen by pranksters and was feared to be lost permanently. Then some six weeks later it was returned anonymously to the pub, amid rumours that the thieves had suffered bad luck. Other tales are told of individuals removing the cat for a joke and then suffering regrettable misfortunes – such as car accidents – shortly afterwards. It has not been possible to verify these tales, which are part of the oral folklore of the town.

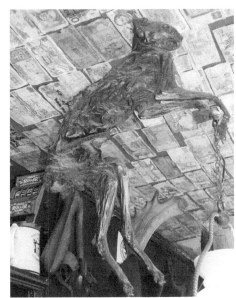

Above left: *The Nutshell.*

Above right: *The mummified cat in the Nutshell.*

The Nutshell has an appropriately pint-sized ghost, a little boy seen upstairs in October 1975. A Mr Sid Frisby, a Nutshell regular, went to the top floor to prepare for a game of dominoes, when he saw the phantom of a small boy sitting alone in the room. The boy vanished before his eyes. Brian Frisby reportedly returned downstairs, looking white and shaking. Brian Wimshurst, the then landlord and his wife, Karin, believed him, as they said that they had felt 'cold shivers' in the upper room.

The cause of the haunting is said to be the spirit of a child who died on the premises in mysterious circumstances. Although the boy has not been seen again, there have been reports of poltergeist disturbances in recent years. In May 2003 staff reported the mysterious shattering of glasses. Various amateur ghost hunting groups have investigated the pub and, in 2004, one group suffered a mysterious draining of batteries in equipment they brought inside with the hope of recording activity.

The former Hardwick Cleaners stood a few doors along the Traverse from the Nutshell. On 21 February 1980 a local paper said that a mischievous spirit of the poltergeist type had been causing havoc there after a new assistant, Mrs Laura Day, started working at the business at the end of 1979. Mrs Shirley Baker was quoted as saying:

He certainly seems to have taken a fancy to Laura. He doesn't seem so friendly to me these days. Last Thursday, for instance, I was hunting for a particular pair of trousers. I went right through the shop, but they were nowhere to be found. Then Laura discovered them right away, hanging on a completely different rail to the one they had been left on.

Mrs Shirley Baker, the manageress, was pressing a skirt when she became aware of, 'a musty smell, like an old church. Then I suddenly felt someone pull me backwards violently. But when I looked round there was no one there.'

The tiny room in which the ghost of a small boy appeared.

Clothes continued to move around the shop, and appear in unusual places. The ghost was also blamed for filling a machine with water and other equipment failures but staff assured customers that the disappearing clothes always turned up again.

St Mary's Church

Set in an extensive churchyard reputedly haunted by the Grey Lady (see Chapter two), St Mary's church is one of the old Abbey churches. Local belief is that the church survived the plundering of the Abbey because it was used by the townspeople. The tower of the church was begun in 1395 and the nave has one of the finest hammer beam roofs in East Anglia, with a flight of carved angels which survived the ravages of the puritan iconoclasts of the seventeenth century. St Mary's church also houses a royal tomb, that of Queen Mary Tudor, and members of the royal family have paid their respects over the years.

Mary Tudor was the second daughter of Henry VIII and the wife of the King Louis XII of France; on the tomb is carved 'Mary, Queen of France, 1533'. Her ghost is said to appear in the church on certain evenings, being glimpsed during services as the light is fading.

The Theatre Royal

Like many theatres around the country, Bury St Edmunds' Theatre Royal is said to be haunted. Built in 1819, the Royal is considered a fine example of a Regency era playhouse, but its charms went ignored for many years. Although the theatre achieved distinction by hosting the first ever performance of the Victorian comedy classic *Charley's Aunt* in 1892, it suffered a much less illustrious period in the twentieth century, being reduced to use as a barrel store by the nearby Greene King brewery for nearly forty years after it closed in 1926. Fortunately, in 1965 the theatre was re-established and restored; further restoration is underway and its future looks assured.

Set within a haunted churchyard, St Mary's has the ghost of Mary Tudor whose tomb is within.

Since it reopened there have been stories of phantom footsteps at the Theatre Royal. These were heard in a side passage by the Theatre Royal's then administrator Mike Saddington and a colleague. Local belief attributes the steps to those of architect William Wilkins who built the theatre, and who was also responsible for the plans for the National Gallery in London. Wilkins had been intent on planning a theatre for Bury St Edmunds from 1808, having first taken a lease of a small theatre above the Market Cross on the Cornhill. The theatre flourished for a period but by the reign of William IV, financial difficulties set in, leading to the first closure of the Theatre Royal in 1843. Two years later the theatre reopened under the direction of William James Achilles Abington. The failure of his pet project and the success enjoyed by Abington is said to have caused the jealous shade of Wilkins to walk.

Recalling his experiences in April 1978, Mike Saddington stated that at one time he would not be in the theatre on his own. Once when present with another person, they heard notes being played from a grand piano kept under the stage. They both rushed downstairs only to find no-one there.

There appear to have been no sightings of Wilkins – if indeed the haunting presence is he – and Mike Saddington stated, 'No-one actually saw it,' and he believed that an exorcism had later taken place. But in August 2004 stories of the haunting were revived when a visiting actress glimpsed a grey shape moving along one the upper circles. It will be interesting to see if the phenomena survive the latest restoration.

Whiting Street

During the First World War, a house near the Masons Arms pub was the scene of poltergeist phenomena. My grandfather, Frederick Mann (1905-1998), recalled hearing about the stories as a boy which involved unexplained knocks and banging sounds and the mysterious levitation of furniture. The stories caused a nine-day wonder and crowds gathered in the hope of witnessing the phenomena. Despite attempts at investigation, no explanation was ever forthcoming and, like many poltergeist outbreaks, it soon faded away.

The haunted Theatre Royal.
(courtesy of Keith Mindham)

Whiting Street with properties
which have experienced ghostly
incidents for over ninety years.

In the summer of 2004 a young mother and her child were living in a flat along Whiting Street and were troubled by what the mother was convinced was a haunting presence. Events culminated in the mother fleeing the property with her child at midnight one night, driven out by the feeling of a menacing presence and an unpleasant chill which was ascribed to a ghost. Fortunately, they were able to swiftly secure housing elsewhere.

A third haunted building in the street is Lloyds the chemist, which stands at the junction with Abbeygate Street. The building incorporates many old timbers from the past and staff have heard the sound of footsteps ascending the stairs when no-one else was in the shop.

FIVE

GHOSTS OF THE BURY ST EDMUNDS DISTRICT

The district surrounding Bury St Edmunds has a great many stories of ghosts and legends of the supernatural, so many that it is not possible to detail or allude to more than a few.

Coldham Hall

Coldham Hall is a spacious seventeenth-century mansion at Stanningfield which briefly became famous on account of its ghost, following the international model Claudia Schiffer and her Hollywood producer husband Matthew Vaughan selecting it as a nuptial home in 2003. Amid the media frenzy surrounding their marriage, stories surfaced of the haunting of Coldham Hall by a ghostly nun called Penelope, a member of the Rookwood family. The Rookwoods had owned Coldham Hall in the 1660s.

These stories first circulated in May 1979, when a retired scrap metal dealer named Richard Duce who had bought the property in the 1950s talked about the haunting in an interview. He stated, 'During the night time there is always something happening in the summer. Sometimes during the day when the sky is bright, the house seems to cloud over'.

He stated that on the walls were two cursed portraits, one believed to be Penelope and another of a mother superior which tradition said should never be taken down. During cleaning and decorating the portraits were moved along the picture rail but never removed from the wall, in case ill-luck should befall the household.

These stories were eagerly picked up in 2003 by the media across Great Britain, the USA and Germany. The Ghost Club made enquiries as to the whereabouts of the pictures without success, but later press stories claimed that Claudia Schiffer and her husband had brought a medium to Coldham Hall to conduct a ceremony of exorcism or deliverance, in an attempt to counteract the haunting. In turn, these stories were subsequently denied, Claudia Schiffer and her husband seemingly preferring to pull a veil across the whole matter.

Left: *One of the mummified cats found in the walls of a cottage at Fakenham Magna in 1972. (courtesy of the* East Anglian Daily Times*)*

Opposite: *Fornham Park haunted by a White Lady and a ghostly monk.*

Fakenham Magna

In August 1972 builders renovating two seventeenth-century cottages at Fakenham Magna were disturbed by manifestations which followed the discovery of five mummified cats and kittens in the walls. The poor animals appeared to have been victims of the old superstitious practice of interring an animal in the walls or foundations of a building as a sacrifice, or a magical protection against witchcraft. Many examples are known in West Suffolk and in other parts of the county (see Chapter three, the Nutshell, Bury St Edmunds).

On one occasion whilst the men were eating their lunch they heard footsteps walking up the path to the cottages, but on looking out there was no-one to be seen. Strange tapping noises were also heard by members of the restoration team, and they complained of an intense, eerie atmosphere. One young workman carried a pick-axe for protection and shortly afterwards quit his job.

One of the builders, Mr John Lomax, took one of the cats back to his home in Ingham to show his wife. It is perhaps no exaggeration to state that Mrs Lomax was not particularly enamoured with this unique treat, but her distaste turned to alarm with the mysterious events which occurred following the arrival of the ancient feline corpse. During the night the couple were disturbed by scratching sounds emanating from a cupboard, as though a live animal was trying to escape. Mr Lomax returned the cat to the cottages the next morning. In August 2003 I spoke to Mrs Lomax about the incidents at her former home in Ingham. She confirmed the noises, adding that she had also been unnerved by the sudden and unexplained fall of a light in the kitchen. The light displaced itself from its fitting without explanation whilst the mummified cat was in their house. Reporters from the *Bury Free Press* who visited the site claimed that the air inside the buildings was 'unnaturally hot'.

The case was investigated by Malcolm Ramplin of Hadleigh, on behalf of the now defunct East Anglian Psychical Research Unit. Members of the group found strange star-shaped carvings on beams which might have been linked to the performance of magic rituals; more interestingly, the group were also reported to have picked up strange tapping noises on a tape recorder.

For a long time, it was believed that the cats were ultimately walled up in the cottages again. However, it emerged in February 2003 that one of the cats had been preserved in Moyses Hall Museum since 1989 and that it was now going on display. Was there some kind of energy or force associated with the mummified bodies which their disturbance unleashed?

Alternatively, were the phenomena triggered by the subconscious minds of one or more of the people involved, one or more of whom were perhaps aware of the association between witches and their animal familiars in folklore?

Fornham St Martin

Until 1930, when a row of bungalows were built upon it, Barton Hill in the parish of Fornham St Martin was a narrow country lane stretching into the countryside with a reputation for being haunted. A year before her death in 1980, a life-long Fornham resident Miss Smith recalled her own ghost experience on the hill, around 1910. As a child she had been walking on Barton Hill with her father. As they walked up the hill they saw the figure of a woman dressed in white clothing approaching them. Initially they thought it was a living person. Miss Smith remembered that the figure seemed to have a white gleam to it, and she noticed that, as it came closer, it glided rather than walked in a normal fashion. There was also was something strange about its pale face and blank expression, which made her think it was not a living person. As it passed by them, the figure suddenly melted away, leaving father and daughter quite alone on the hillside.

Shaken by what they had witnessed, neither spoke of their strange experience until they reached home. On discussing what they had seen, and on comparing their descriptions, they realised that they had both seen the same spectral figure. Miss Smith remembered that her father had been greatly disturbed by the apparition and told his daughter never to speak of it again. Miss Smith grew up to run the village shop for many years but never told anyone of her experience until relaying it to me, following a talk I gave to the village over-sixties club in 1979.

Interestingly, another long-standing Fornham resident, the late Mrs Day, knew a curious story about Barton Hill which circulated in the early years of the twentieth century. At midnight the ghost of a white dog was supposed to run down the hill and then vanish into the meadow at the bottom near a small stream. Mrs Day recalled that her uncle believed he had seen the ghost. He lodged with Mrs Day and her husband in the village during the early 1920s. One night he arrived home shaking, declaring, 'I've seen the dog!'. The cause of the apparition was said to lie in accident many years before on the hill. The site had been unwisely chosen by a lady learning to a ride a bicycle on Barton Hill who had lost control of the machine and collided with a fence at the bottom of the hill, with fatal results. Local tradition thereafter averred that the hill was haunted by the dog which represented the transmogrified spirit of the lady; an interesting example of the survival of the belief in the spirit of human being returning after death in the guise of a phantom animal.

Fornham Park

Fornham Park is one of the most interesting and atmospheric green spaces near Bury St Edmunds, yet remains a curiously isolated and little-known place. Surrounded by thick woodland, it has been largely forgotten by local people and historians alike, despite it being the site of an important battle. On 17 October 1173, forces loyal to King Henry II routed a rebel army composed largely of Flemish mercenaries led by the Earl of Leicester. Townspeople of Bury St Edmunds joined the closing skirmishes of the battle, believing themselves aided by St Edmund and taking the opportunity for plunder. Many of the dead were buried where they lay; during the nineteenth century a large barrow was unearthed and found to contain over thirty skeletons. Local folklore avers that other casualties were buried in barrows as far away as Ingham, but these mounds were in fact Bronze Age interments.

The park also contained a thatched Norman church dedicated to St Genevieve and was later the site of an imposing manor house. During the mid-eighteenth century the park was landscaped as a large and scenic garden. Unfortunately, the thatched church was burned down in June 1775 by a local man out shooting rooks or jackdaws, the shot setting alight to the roof. The church was never rebuilt and today only the tower remains, reminiscent of Glastonbury Tor, a monolithic structure against the horizon. The former graveyard – some distance away on the edge of a golf course – continued to be used for another century before being abandoned, and is now virtually obliterated.

Local tradition says that the ruin is haunted on Christmas Eve night by the ghost of a monk, possibly involved with the battle in 1173. It was not unknown for monks to be attached as chaplains in medieval armies or even taking up arms. Alternatively, the figure could be one of the Benedictine brothers from St Edmunds Abbey who administered last rites to the dying in

All that remains of the gates of Fornham Park haunted by an entity known as 'Red Hannah'.

the aftermath of the battle, the fate of the soul after violent death being a particular concern during the twelfth century.

Fornham Hall remained an imposing manor house until the Second World War when the site was taken over by the army. First used as a camp for Indian soldiers, it was later used as a POW camp and then as a training ground for the military. The landscaped park was largely obliterated in the process, with the exception of some fine cedar trees, and the damage was further compounded by mineral extraction after the hall was demolished in 1950. All that remained was a stable block which has recently been renovated after standing derelict for many years.

Shortly before demolition of the hall, soldiers based at the building reported seeing the figure of a woman dressed in white. She appeared at midnight, walking from the house out into the park past the church tower and towards the lake. Like many White Lady apparitions her identity is a mystery, but she does not appear to have been the only female ghost reputed to haunt the area. At the turn of the twentieth century, folklore also averred that the gates of the park were haunted by a female phantom. The ghost was a local bogey known as 'Red Hannah' who was used to scare naughty village children. Red Hannah was said to appear at dusk near the entrance to the park between the Fornham and Ingham crossroads, now occupied by a roundabout. Today, only a solitary pillar remains but it is interesting to note that nocturnal visitors to the park have also encountered an unpleasant atmosphere around the spot.

The site of the former crossroads, now transformed into a roundabout, was the scene of a strange experience by two local men just after the Second World War. In 1979, the late Mr Boast of Fornham St Martin recalled that in 1946 he had been walking one evening with a friend towards the crossroads. Both men heard the sound of a motorbike fast-approaching from the direction of Ingham, although they could see no lights or any machine or rider. The sound ceased suddenly and they had the impression that there had been a crash. On reaching the spot they found nothing. Both then recalled that about a year had passed since a young man riding a motorbike had been involved with a crash and sustained fatal head injuries, dying at the spot. Despite scorn from those who heard the story, Mr Boast remained convinced he and his companion had both heard a re-enactment of the fatal crash, and the sound of a phantom motorbike.

Hengrave Hall.

For folklorists, the location of this experience is an interesting one. Since classical times, crossroads have been considered uncanny places, the myths of ancient Greece holding them sacred to Hecate, goddess of witches. The belief that crossroads hold a peculiar attraction for supernatural entities is found in many European cultures and in England their uncanny reputation was undoubtedly fuelled by their choice until the early nineteenth century as the burial place for suicides. It is also noticeable that ghost lore worldwide often invests the meeting points of various kinds of man-made or natural boundaries with supernatural significance, and the parish boundary is near the site.

Hengrave Hall

This large and ornate sixteenth-century hall has recently returned to private hands after falling revenues and prohibitive health and safety costs resulted in its closure from use as a Christian educational centre and, formerly, a Catholic school. The once moated hall was built between 1525-38 by Sir Thomas Kitson, laid out upon a quadrangular plan and incorporating many novel Italian-style features.

I first enquired about ghosts at the hall on a visit by members of St George's church, in Bury St Edmunds, in the summer of 1977, to be told that no ghostly phenomena had been recognised at the hall beyond a few strange noises sometimes heard at night. However, such was the size and age of the property, the custodian felt that these were likely to be the wind or just imagination embellishing naturally occurring sounds. Certainly, stories of ghosts at Hengrave Hall were always played down during its time as a school, but more recent accounts aver that it was haunted by a female apparition in a pink dress, known as 'the Pink Lady'. On one occasion in the 1990s the Pink Lady was said to have manifested in a bedroom to a surprised adult guest and then seen to glide through the room and then, seconds later, to float out through a window.

The haunted Plough Inn.

Icklingham

Lying eight miles north north-west of Bury St Edmunds, the village of Icklingham has long had a reputation for being haunted. The Temple Bridge at Icklingham is said to be haunted by one of the most archetypal ghost figures, a headless horseman. This tradition may be a folk memory of an event that took place near here in 1381. During Wat Tyler's rebellion, the rebels were seeking John de Cambridge, the prior (deputy abbot) of the house. He was apprehended at Icklingham and beheaded. His head was taken in triumph to Bury, and his body lay untended for five days.

A mound by a side road, about a mile north of Temple Bridge, is known as 'Deadman's Grave'. Tradition holds that a man died in a riding accident here, and was buried on the spot; an alternative story claims he was a highwayman. Angered that he had been denied Christian burial, his ghost haunted the spot, rising from the grave to terrify passing horses and cattle so they could not keep to the path. Henry Prigg (who later changed his name to Trigg), author of the *Icklingham Papers* and a local archaeologist, excavated the spot at the end of the nineteenth century, but found nothing.

A spot to the east of All Saints' church was avoided in the nineteenth century when locals said that it marked a 'witches' path'. It was said that a gap in the hedge here could never be closed, and after dark there were uncanny forms. In particular, there were reports of a ghostly white rabbit disappearing through the opening. The reputation of the spot was confirmed when a Roman cemetery was found on the site in 1871; two stone coffins were later exhibited at Moyses Hall. The story of the rabbit is still known in the village – boosted by the occasional appearance of albino rabbits or escaped domestic animals. The story may have its origins in the belief that witches were able to transform themselves into hares, whilst in parts of the Breckland near Thetford, the dreaded Black Shuck, the archetypal phantom hound of East Anglia, was said to take on the guise of a rabbit with flaming eyes.

Not all Icklingham ghosts are confined to folklore. In December 1996 Mrs Brenda King, the landlady at the Plough Inn, reported seeing a 'cloaked figure' in the pub (which had formerly been cottages). What is now part of the car park was once a gravel pit. Three customers had also seen the figure.

In April 1997, I visited Brenda King at the Plough. She had lived at the pub with her husband since 1992 and she confirmed the sighting was one of a number of curious incidents. Both she and a number of her customers felt a presence in the pub, particularly concentrated in a passageway leading out of the toilets, which was then reached through a door in the restaurant extension, added in the 1950s. Brenda stated that she normally never had any worries about being in the pub at night, or walking about the premises in the dark, with the exception of this passageway. Her feeling was shared by the King family's dog, which was observed to growl at the spot, and which refused to go down the passageway, as though it could sense something unpleasant.

One evening in the summer of 1993 Brenda King was walking down the passageway when she felt that she had walked into something 'like cobwebs'. Just as she became aware of this peculiar sensation she saw a shadow or silhouette of a figure in a black cloak, but both the figure and the creepy sensation vanished after a few seconds. However, this did not perturb her.

A barmaid called Teresa recalled how she had encountered the same sensation of somebody or something brushing past her in the bar. Teresa had the sensation that it might be an animal, as the feeling of being touched was against her lower legs.

It is sometimes the case that publicans exaggerate their ghosts and court publicity in the hope that it will attract extra trade but, if anything, Mr and Mrs King had hitherto played down the occurrences at the Plough out of natural reluctance for being made the target of such suggestions.

On occasions bells in the bar and the kitchen had rung repeatedly without explanation. Although it might be thought that a person was responsible, they were unable to catch him or her. Such incidents might be due to a fault in the electric wiring or power supply, but it was harder to explain the repeated setting off of the smoke alarm in the spring of 1996, as there was no battery in the alarm. These were attributed to the work of the 'ghost'. In fact, these odd incidents are identical to many haunted pubs across Britain which report the moving or breaking glasses or ashtrays, tampering with beer taps and barrels, the touching of bar staff and curious sounds. So typical is this pattern of phenomena within licensed premises that it would not be excessive to speak of the Plough being an example of 'haunted pub syndrome'.

The family who ran the Plough before the Kings said that lights would switch on and off in the building. This family had also run a bed & breakfast service, and once in the 1980s they recalled that two lorry drivers had been so alarmed by the lights continually switching on and off that they left, fearful of staying the night. Under this family's tenancy, other customers had experienced the sensation of a figure brushing past them, one while seated in the bar, another while standing near the bar counter.

In June 2006 I visited the Plough again and discovered it had changed hands once more and had been renovated and given an extended dining area. Quite often substantial building work may put pay to manifestations for a period and it appears that phenomena no longer reach the intensity of the 1990s. However, one of the bar staff confirmed that she had experienced the sensation of being touched in the six weeks since she had begun working in the pub, so it may be that an active presence continues to manifest.

Risby

A strange light was seen over the rooftops of the village of Risby on 18 August 1783 and reported in the *Bury Post* for 28 August that year. The principal witness was Mr Amyss, the keeper of the White Horse Inn, who stated he was looking out of his ground floor window when he, 'saw a great light in the horizon, seemingly over Cavenham'. He called his family to witness the light, which seemed to be proceeding towards his house. It had a bluish colour and, when about a quarter of mile away, it was seen to shed a quantity of stars. It came close to his house and, 'as he thought just clear of the chimneys' before heading off in the direction of Saxham. Mr Amyss estimated the object to be between 16-17ft across. This may have been the same object which a witness on the Angel Hill had seen the same evening break into three distinct bodies and also shedding stars which seemed to fall. Other reports were received from Ixworth, and as far as way as Sudbury, all of which seemed to have described a similar object. Official interpretations classed the object as a meteor but the behaviour of the object, including its low altitude and relatively slow speed, seem to preclude this.

More traditional spectres have also been noted in the village. During the early 1950s a Bury St Edmunds lady, Mrs Pamment, was walking with a group of teenage friends through the village after a night out. As she walked down the dark village street, she witnessed what she believed to be a ghostly figure in white glide in front of them and disappear through the window of a house near the village hall. One wonders if this could be connected with the apparition of a man, 'looking like a country gentleman of the late Georgian or early Victorian period' who walks up the road by Risby church. Local stories state that a former rector's son once spoke to him whereupon he vanished away.

In November 1979, the late Mrs Hardy of Risby described to me her sighting of the figure of an old country woman, apparently collecting sticks, in a copse near her home. Mrs Hardy was convinced she was an apparition. Another ghost was seen on the outskirts of the village, on the modern slip road on to the A14 in February 2002 by a man from Bury St Edmunds. He was parked on the slip road about midnight when he saw a human figure and dog walking along the road towards him. According to the account he gave me, the figure resembled an old man in dark clothing but the facial features were unclear, and both apparitions vanished as they drew close to the car.

Rushbroooke Hall

Rushbrooke Hall was a fine Elizabethan building which was badly damaged by fire in 1961 and demolished in 1973. Today, only a few walls and the moat remain, but it is this now small and denuded patch of water which is traditionally the scene of the haunting.

The earliest published account of the ghost of Rushbrooke Hall appears to have been by the Victorian writer Augustus Hare in *The Story of My Life* (1900). An inveterate society gossip and traveller, Augustus Hare recorded a visit at the end of September 1886 and his account gives the impression that the lady was Henrietta Maria but this is incorrect:

> On Monday we picnicked at the park of Penseroo, the old house of Rushbrooke, standing in a wide moat, into which a former mistress of the place is said to float nightly. Her picture hangs above the magnificent staircase, and the window whence she was thrown is pointed out

Rushbrooke Hall in 1937.

at the end of a suite of desolate unfurnished rooms. The house belonged to Lord Jermyn, and whatever his relation to Henrietta Maria may have, two magnificent cabinets of hers are here, which Lord Bristol, to his despair, inadvertently sold, with the house, to its present possessors.

The reference to Henrietta Maria is Queen Henrietta Maria, but she certainly did not drown in the moat at Rushbrooke. The more likely candidate for the identity of the White Lady appears in *Haunted Houses* (1924) by Charles Harper who gives the name of the ghostly lady as one Agnes de Rushbrooke.

Most ghost book writers have done little more than copy these references from Hare and Harper, although veteran ghost hunter Peter Underwood did reveal more about the haunting in his autobiography *No Common Task* (1983) based upon personal enquiry and experience. Whilst on military service in Suffolk during the Second World War, Peter Underwood stayed at the Hall in 1941 and learned that the manifestation was said to occur on a particular night of the year in the summer (unfortunately he does not state the actual date). During the course of the night on the anniversary of the supposed murder, listeners were rewarded by a loud splash from the moat which was attributed to the ghost.

The Society for Psychical Research holds a letter from 1889 recording phenomena experienced at the hall during the tenancy of the Vansittart family in 1854. The account in the letter is second hand but extremely detailed. Among many incidents which frightened both servants and occupants was the sound of footsteps following them down the stairs.

Research locally has confirmed that the Vansittart family rented Rushbrooke Hall during the earliest 1850s. If so, this must be the earliest recorded haunting at the hall and is a reminder that even an obscure folkloric tale may actually have a basis in factual events in the past.

The haunted moat at Rushbrooke Hall.

Rougham

In November 1989, the story of a ghost allegedly starting a fire in a cottage in Rougham made international news. The ghost was said to have struck on a number of occasions at one of the Spinney Cottages, occupied by a family of three.

Christine Arnold, forty-eight, was reported to have been taken to hospital after a fire which broke out in a cupboard and destroyed clothes within, as well as causing smoke damage to the rest of the cottage. A pet parrot died as a result of the fire which ignited whilst Christine and her daughter Sarah, seventeen, and Sarah's boyfriend Paul Jupp, twenty-one, were out.

A few days later Sarah heard a voice saying, 'That was funny, wasn't it?' which she believed was a reference to the fire. She told the local *Bury Free Press*, 'I thought it was my mother speaking but when I turned round I realised it could not have been. It was a strange voice – almost as if it was trying to imitate my mother'. On another occasion she felt as though she had been pushed as she stood at her sink. According to her boyfriend, she had been left, 'as white as a sheet after the incident'.

The family had moved into the rented cottage in June 1988 and experienced what were described as, '… a string of ghostly happenings'. It seems the phenomena seemed to have a sense of timing with events breaking out particularly around 9.20 p.m. which they estimated was approximately the time fire started. On two occasions priests were called in to sprinkle holy water but these failed to calm the disturbances.

Paul Jupp stated, 'They concentrated around a tree in the garden and also the cupboard where the fire was later discovered. The vicar actually said he had a bad feeling about the cupboard. He thought something might be in there.'

Bizarre though these incidents might be they are not without precedent in poltergeist literature. Poltergeists have been blamed for starting fires on occasion; mysterious outbreaks of fire were reported in the Enfield poltergeist case in 1977-79. Incendiary poltergeists have been relatively little studied in the UK but many cases have been documented in the USA. A writer on psychic topics, the late Vincent Gaddis, in his book *Mysterious Fires and Lights* (1966), considered:

> There is a definite relationship between electrical phenomena and mediumship plus psychical phenomena in general. Accounts of luminous appearances and lights, ranging from pin-points to globular forms of a foot or so in diameter, have appeared in séance reports. During other periods of other phenomena there have been changes in the intensity of electrical currents in buildings.

Gaddis considered that poltergeist agents might store minute electrical energy in their bodies which might then produce or manipulate electrical forces to cause fires.

In a small number of poltergeist cases, the phenomenon seems to develop a human-sounding voice or is associated with auditory hallucinations experienced by members of a household. The failure of ritual ceremonies to disperse the energy is explicable if it is recognised that the events were of a poltergeist nature, the majority of which appear to be generated by the subconscious minds of living agents.

The story of the Rougham cottage was widely reported and in the United States, one American investigator named Larry Arnold (no relation) mentioned the story in his book *Ablaze!* (1996) considering that the case might even shed light on the enigma of so-called spontaneous human combustion. However, this was pure speculation, the phenomena of SHC being considered dubious at best. Certainly, there is nothing in the literature of psychical research to suggest anything as dramatic actually takes place in poltergeist cases and examples of poltergeists ever harming residents of affected premises are exceedingly rare. Often the most dramatic incidents represent a peak in events, after which the disturbances subside and this may be what happened with the Rougham case as no further incidents were reported.

Rougham Airfield

The Rougham Aerodrome was one of many which dotted East Anglia during the Second World War and was a base for the American Airforce, the Eight Airforce and the 94th bomb group flying B17s. Airmen stationed at Rougham suffered some 2,000 casualties with between 500 and 1,000 fatalities.

After the Second World War the control tower was lived in by the Manager for the Ministry of Agriculture and used for storage of food stuffs for misplaced persons and for the Berlin airlift. One building continued to be occupied as a private home for a long period afterwards but by the late 1980s the site had become derelict. Today the former aerodrome largely consists of Nissen huts and hangars now on edge of an industrial estate but amongst survivors are the mortuary and a restored control room.

Ghost stories began circulating about the airfield in the early 1970s. In around 1971 a local craftsman named Stoveld is said to have been working in an old hangar one morning and was surprised to hear the sound of an aircraft taking off. There was nothing to be seen.

In 1992 the Rougham Tower Association was founded by a local man, David Hardy, who wanted to see the site restored into a museum and war memorial, and he served as chairman of the organisation for a number of years. Since the RTA was established, the old airfield has been used for aerial displays but plans for a truly fitting museum and regular flying displays have been thwarted by the construction of a large housing estate nearby.

Over the years David Hardy has collected a number of stories about ghosts at the site, as well as having first-hand experience of strange sounds himself. Soon after the RTA was founded, David Hardy recalls being at work with a colleague, Mick Clay, in the pilot's ready room, stripping down paint. It was early on a snowy November evening and no-one else was around. David Hardy recalls, 'We heard what sounded like a car radio, muted voices talking, and we thought, someone's turned up. We heard voices and they seemed pretty close, so we went outside. No car, no people, no anything. Yet definitely there was a conversation going on'.

Other stories have told of the sound of engines, and a ghostly officer in pinks standing on the parapet looking out to the airfield. Another story has a phantom of a pilot dragging a parachute towards the tower, close to the hedge on the site. One story is that the ghost is a casualty from an aircraft which crashed after running out of fuel, whilst awaiting permission to land. According to one story the pilot is said to be heard pitifully crying, 'Why wouldn't you let us land?' but no first-hand witness has been traced.

In August 2001 I was one of a group of nine people who conducted a vigil at the aerodrome. Five participants were members of the Ghost Club and four were connected with the RTA and interested in the accounts of ghosts. In particular, one was the fiancée of one of the RTA members, and a lady who was training to be a medium who was interested in picking up impressions from the site. During a preliminary inspection of the tower, whilst in the control room, I had a strong mental impression of happy atmosphere, and of voices and laughter. I did not mention this but later the trainee medium stated she picked up happy voices and laughter in the same area. Since this seemed to be a subjective experience on my part, I am tempted to ascribe it to auto-suggestion, perhaps induced by a subconscious interpretation of noises arising from unusually soft and flexible floorboards (eucalyptus wood) of the control room which creaked as people moved about. Alternatively, it might have been a case of telepathy or a genuine psychic impression. However, no other unusual incidents occurred during the night, and various experiments involving trigger objects and planchette communications, produced no results.

Nonetheless, many members of the RTA still consider that the tower is haunted. Are there unquiet spirits? Perhaps, or perhaps what witnesses perceive are the echoes of the concentrated emotions and feelings which characterised life at the airfield during the stressful days and nights of wartime.

Westley

Westley is a small and unspoilt village two miles west of Bury St Edmunds, currently under threat from plans for housing expansion. Often overlooked, it appears Westley has been a settlement for many centuries, for prehistoric and Roman remains have been found there. It may also have been the scene of strange UFO-like manifestations, perhaps similar to the strange lights seen at Risby, for a seventeenth-century parish register recorded 'three suns' being 'seene by men of good credit in the space of one whole hower [hour]' in 1614.

Nestling on the very western edge of the village of Westley at the end of Church Lane is all that remains of the long-ruined church of St Thomas à Becket and thirteen gravestones from the old graveyard. Local stories say the area around the church is haunted by a White Lady who appears on the first day of every month. Like so many apparitions her identity is a mystery but the overgrown church is the perfect background for such a manifestation.

West Stow Hall

West Stow Hall is a privately owned ancient house with a fine brick gatehouse with four polygonal turrets. Built in around 1520 by Sir John Crofts, Master of the Horse for Mary Tudor, the gatehouse was later extended by a passageway to the hall which has a number of interesting features. In one upper room there is a wall painting reflecting the Elizabethan taste for poignant reminders of mortality and the transient nature of human life and happiness. It depicts a man hunting saying, 'Thus do I do all day'; a lover says, 'Thus do I while I may'; an old man looking at the lover and his lady says, 'Thus did I when I might'; and an even more decrepit figure says, 'Good Lord, will this world last forever?'.

The hall reputedly has a Grey Lady who may be the ghost of a girl supposedly murdered by her lover at some time in the past. The room thereafter became haunted, but details are sparse. During the early part of the twentieth century, West Stow Hall was unoccupied for a period and enjoyed a lively reputation for being haunted. Local stories described a remarkably physical ghost which could produce unusual poltergeist tricks and was even said to have struck a would-be investigator on one occasion. One particular story collected by the Cambridge folklorist, the late Enid Porter, and told in the district for many years, held that a local man had agreed to stay in the haunted room overnight for a wager. His vantage point must have proved rather comfortable, for as he sat alone in the darkened hall he found himself nodding off and was soon asleep. Halfway through the night he was awoken by the feeling of a stinging slap against his cheek. On examining his face the next day in the mirror, he saw a red mark about the size of a palm upon one cheek, a mark which did not fade for several weeks.

Right: *A ghostly White Lady walks at the ruined church at Westley on the first day of every month.*

Opposite: *The overgrown ruin of St Thomas à Becket's church, Westley.*

Another contemporary story averred that the kitchen was haunted and that a bowl danced in the sink every night. This story reached the ears of Prince Duleep Singh, who owned Elveden Hall in the nineteenth and early twentieth centuries, and was interested in English folklore and psychical phenomena. He relayed it in a talk to the Suffolk Archaeological Society in 1901. It was taken sufficiently seriously for the local historian and author Horace Barker to enquire about the ghost for his book *West Suffolk Illustrated* (1907) when the hall was again occupied. On asking about the phenomena he received a dismissive one-word answer, 'Rats!'. Pondering the meaning of the reply, Barker considered the word had been, '… used in its literal sense and not as a colloquial term of scepticism and derision.'

Wordwell Hall, Wordwell

Wordwell is a hamlet north of Bury St Edmunds which has never recovered from the Black Death. Around 1999, Mrs Rhoda Titlestad visited Wordwell Hall with her cousin and her husband and stayed with the owners, as she had done many times before. After a day out, she retired close to midnight, her bedroom being one with old oak beams and a tiny window. In a vivid letter describing her experience, Rhoda wrote to me, 'Just before getting into bed, I crossed the room to pull back the curtains and open the window. Midway, I collided with a "presence". I can only describe it as similar to a severe electric shock. There was a reddish glow around me and the aired chilled. Naturally, I was scared!' Rhoda Titlestad timidly apologised to the 'presence' and retreated to bed and then pulled the duvet around herself.

West Stow Hall, c.1809.

The next morning Rhoda recounted her experience to her host, and asked, 'Were there spirits in the house?' He replied, 'We do have a ghost' and went on to inform Rhoda but said he had not told her, 'because other visitors have declined to return after being told'. He said his father had often had an experience which he ascribed to the ghost touching his shoulder. The ghost was considered to be the spirit of a girl who had been murdered in one of the oldest parts of the house – where Rhoda had been sleeping. Rhoda had stayed in the room many times before and on occasions since but has not had a similar encounter.

However, such experiences are not unknown. The veteran journalist and founder of *Panorama*, the late Dennis Bardens (1911-2004), told me of two personal experiences of a similar nature, two of a number of ghostly incidents which he encountered during his long life. The first occurred in a flat in Highgate in the 1930s when he suddenly witnessed a strange electrical glow which illuminated the room and then disappeared. He described this experience in his book *Ghosts and Hauntings* (1965). His second encounter with the glow took place over sixty years later, whilst in his late eighties when staying for a short break at a residential centre for writers and artists at Mount Pleasant in Surrey. Both manifestations occurred late at night and in bedrooms and gave the impression of a luminous, dynamic presence of an electrical nature. In neither case could Dennis Bardens propose any explanation for the incidents which, despite his great knowledge and experience of psychic matters, remained a puzzle to him until the end of his life.

SIX

M.R. JAMES AND THE MOST HAUNTED VILLAGE IN ENGLAND

It is a singularly appropriate coincidence that the writer universally acclaimed as the creator of the finest fictional ghost stories in English should have grown up in what is the most haunted village in Suffolk and, perhaps, the most haunted village in England. From the age of three and through his boyhood, Montague Rhodes James (1862-1936) lived at the old Rectory at Great Livermere, five miles north of Bury St Edmunds. Originally his stories were confined to a small, select gathering of students and fellows at King's College, Cambridge where James spent much of his adult life as a fellow, dean and ultimately provost. Over a century on, his stories have achieved a worldwide circulation, having been endlessly reprinted and anthologised ever since. Truly deserving of the status of classics, their appeal has crossed generations and seems to exert ever greater fascination upon readers as the years go by. But few realise that his earliest ideas about ghosts and the supernatural were formed in this still isolated village, features of which he was later to incorporate in some of his stories which are celebrated today as the finest example of the whole genre.

Great Livermere takes its name from a long serpentine stretch of water, perhaps once the site of votive offerings during the Iron Age, although it was channelled by local landowners in the nineteenth century. Great Livermere has often been mentioned in guidebooks and from as long ago as the 1820s noted as a beautiful area but one which is either missed or overlooked with corresponding frequency because of its sprawling geography. As a traveller's guide stated in 1970, 'The church and the small village are lost on side roads seldom traversed by visitors' and this remains very much the position today. To go into Great Livermere is to enter a village which still has an isolated feel and an atmosphere conducive to thoughts and impressions of ghosts.

M.R. James and Great Livermere

Montague Rhodes James was born in Kent, the son of a clergyman. In 1865, at the age of two the family moved to Great Livermere in Suffolk where his father took up the post of rector until his death in 1909.

In his academic life, M.R. James was a distinguished medieval scholar and author of what remains the leading study of the apocryphal books of the Bible. It was at Livermere Rectory, to the east of the park, that he first developed his life-long interest in ancient history and old manuscripts. He began with studying and sketching old churches and buildings near his home, a leaning that first emerged in his school holidays and eventually resulted in what still remains one of the best books available on Norfolk and Suffolk churches. In 1903 he organised an archaeological excavation of the Chapter House in Bury St Edmunds Abbey. The finds were presented to the Bury St Edmunds Museum and are considered amongst the most important medieval exhibits.

However, it is his thirty fictional short stories about ghosts for which his name endures. Most were written after 1893 when he became dean of King's College, Cambridge. With the appointment he became responsible for the fabric of the chapel, doubtless close to his heart. It was whilst the holder of this office that he began a tradition of reading ghost stories aloud to friends and scholars at candlelit gatherings in the Wilkins building at Christmas time.

A number of his classic stories have an East Anglian setting, which may have been prefigured by an earlier attempt at a ghost story book involving both M.R. James and his brother. This was a fictional work called *Bogey Tales of East Anglia*, published in 1891. The precise authorship cannot be ascertained but the prevailing opinion is that James and his brother were responsible. More potent influences are likely to have been superstitions in Great Livermere where a belief in witches persisted, his father finding occasion to condemn the, 'quasi-religious belief of some who have esoteric confidence in witchcraft in the village'. A visit to an old library at Monks Eleigh church in Suffolk inspired a tale entitled *Canon Alberic's Scrapbook* in which a student called Dennistoun visits a church and finds manuscripts illustrated with horrifying monsters. As

Right: *M.R. James at King's College, Cambridge.*

Opposite: *Great Livermere church where M.R. James's father was rector.*

his research progresses, Dennistoun realises that the illustrations are not simply artistic creations. M.R. James read this to the Chitchat Club, an informal university society. The response was so enthusiastic that a story reading by James became an annual tradition. When James entered the room all the candles except one would be extinguished and he would sit down 'to expound his latest tale to the enthralled gathering'.

After several years, James was urged to publish his stories and in 1904 the first – and now highly sought-after volume *Ghost Stories of an Antiquary* appeared. A second collection followed in 1911. From their appearance, praise for the stories was high. At first it came from James's friends, one of whom wrote, 'You have succeeded in giving me two bad nights and one jumpy walk on a foggy evening in the country when every tree became possessed of horrible long arms and every step was dogged by hideous echoes about ten yards behind.' Such feelings were soon shared by critics and connoisseurs of ghost stories.

Their success as stories results from the skilful creation of atmosphere. M.R. James adopted a restrained, antiquarian tone reflecting the scholarly and erudite world in which he spent his entire adult life. Many of his human characters are male scholars and academics into whose dry, bookish lives James progressively introduces manifestations by malevolent and physically dangerous ghosts. Classic stories include *O Whistle and I'll come to you, Count Magnus, Lost Hearts, The Treasure of Abbot Thomas* and *Number 13*, in which the reader is terrified by the use of suggestion rather than explicit horror.

Two of his best stories involve ghosts from Scandinavia, including *Count Magnus* in which spectres from a padlocked tomb follow their victim back from Sweden to 'Belchamp St Pauls' in Essex (based on the Belchamp villages on the Suffolk/Essex border). But it was places in Suffolk which were used to even greater effect.

In what is probably his most famous story *O Whistle and I'll Come to You*, a Cambridge don is haunted by a spirit he calls up when blowing an antique whistle found in an ancient Templar preceptory on the coast at 'Burstow', modelled upon Felixstowe. The Aldeburgh area became 'Seaburgh' in a *Warning to the Curious*, a story involving three buried crowns, an element so convincing that it has become part of the folklore of the district. However, it is with the setting for the ghastly supernatural events in *The Ash Tree* that M.R. James was writing about Great Livermere.

The important sites in the story are listed as being the 'square block of white house, older inside than out, park with fringe of woods and mere' which represents a thinly disguised Livermere Hall and its surroundings. The story concerns the curse of a woman executed for witchcraft who uses the mechanism of giant spiders dwelling in an ash tree as the instrument of her revenge against the local squire and his descendents. The name of the witch is Mothersole, a village name which appears in the local burial register for Great Livermere. In the story she is hanged after a trial at Bury St Edmunds, 'up the rough grass hill outside Northgate' where indeed witches were put to death in the seventeenth century. Doubtless the horrible familiars of the witch, the veinous spiders, 'the size of a man's head', that live within the ash tree of the title and emerge at night to slay the living have their origins in smaller specimens which would have been common in the country; it is generally accepted that James had a strong dislike of arachnids.

From their first appearance the stories were enthusiastically reviewed, and James continued to write ghost stories into the 1930s, although there is nothing in his later output which really matches his first two collections. In 1919 he left Cambridge to take up the position of Provost at Eton which he had attended some forty years before. Along with many other tasks he sat upon the entrance examination board. Among candidates was a young Christopher Lee who was later to find international fame as an actor playing many of the most dreadful villains of fantasy and supernatural literature in their cinematic depiction in the horror films made by Hammer between the 1950s and 1970s; Lee recalled James in 1977 as, '... a charming man who, as the stories suggest, very much fitted the image of the scholar.'

Right: *An advertisement for a collection of M.R. James stories from the 1930s.*

Opposite left: *Many of James's characters are male scholars and academics whose dry, bookish lives are disturbed by malevolent and physically dangerous ghosts.*

Opposite right: *M.R. James at his desk at Eton, c.1925.*

For his own part, James had a set of ground rules for ghost stories. He considered fictional stories should be intelligibly written and contain no verbose occult symbolism. The background should be the mundane everyday world, to make their build-ups more frightening. For his own part he considered the nineteenth-century Irish writer Sheridan Le Fanu to be the greatest exponent of the literary ghost story. James was willing to explain what he considered to be the rules of the genre to a wider audience, doing so in an essay entitled 'Stories I have tried to write'. In another work he stated James was not without a strong sense of humour, some of which penetrates his stories and which would have been apparent to his audience when the tales were read aloud. The one thing he felt incompatible with the ghost story was sex.

By the 1920s and 1930s it seems that James was prepared to acknowledge the popular acclaim which had by then attached to his fictions, and began to write more openly about them, although one gets the impression that many of his real inspirations and motivations may have been suppressed or concealed. He admitted that he sought to make his fictional ghosts consistent with the spectres of supernatural folklore and declared that he prepared to accept the evidence for ghosts if convincing. It is clear that he delved into contemporary stories of ghosts – hoping in particular that the spectres described by the Irish ghost hunter Elliot O'Donnell were not true – as well as taking a scholarly interest in historic ghost stories, translating a number from medieval Latin manuscripts.

It must be stated that enjoyable as such stories are, they thankfully bear little or no real resemblance to genuine manifestations which psychical researchers and ghost hunters have been documenting for over a century. Although an encounter with a real apparition can generate puzzlement, alarm and even fear in the witness, the shocks are generally not serious or long-lasting. Nor is there any good reason to attribute consciousness, let alone any intention – malevolent or otherwise – to the vast majority of apparitions. Most ghosts seem to cause no real problems at all, and even those seemingly most able to disrupt the actual physical environment – the poltergeists – rarely inflict any harm or injury on members of the households in which they erupt. To be strictly fair to James, when he wrote that ghosts were to be consistent with the

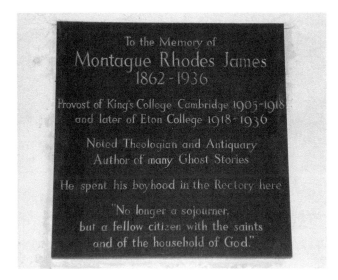

The plaque to M.R. James dedicated in September 1998 at Great Livermere church.

rules of folklore, he was as much drawing upon his knowledge of Scandinavian lore, rather than recorded British traditions or testimony gathered by psychic research groups. In other cases, his stories may have developed from dreams, or possibly even a childhood experience. These would have occurred in the isolated Livermere rectory which was in many senses the real home of M.R. James for forty-four years, the family connection not being severed until 1909.

His output of stories dwindled by the end of the 1920s and James died at Eton School on 12 June 1936, the anniversary of his father's death, as the words of the *Nunc Dimittis*, 'Lord, now lettest thy servant depart in peace: according to thy word' were being sung in chapel. He was buried three days later in the town cemetery. His last story *A Vignette* was published posthumously, and is often omitted from collections of his work; it has a strongly personal feel and is the only one of his stories to have been told in the first person. James's biographer Michael Cox believed the setting was Great Livermere and that it had, 'an autobiographical flavour'.

In September 1998 a special service of evensong to give thanks for the life of M.R. James was held at Great Livermere church and a plaque was dedicated to his memory. Arranged by members of the Ghost Story Society and attended by the nephew of the writer, the service also included a masterly reading by Roger Johnson of *A Vignette*. The selection was stimulated by the growing view of many critics and researchers that both his interest in ghosts and his last story had been inspired by a childhood experience or nightmare. In *A Vignette* James writes of a gate with a square hole cut in it, and how one afternoon, looking from the house towards the gate:

> Through that hole I could see – and it struck like a blow on the diaphragm – something white or partly white. Now this I could not bear – and with an excess of something like courage – only it was more like desperation, like determining I must know the worst – I did steal down and, quite uselessly of course, taking cover behind bushes as I went, I made progress until I was within range of the gate and the hole. Things were, alas! Worse than I had feared. Through that hole a face was looking my way. It was not monstrous, not pale, fleshless, spectral. Malevolent I thought and think it was; at any rate the eyes were large and open and fixed. It was pink and, I thought hot, and just above the eyes the border of a white linen drapery hung down from the

Beryl Dyson who has chronicled the ghosts of Great Livermere.

brows… I fled, but at what I thought must be a safe distance inside my own precincts I could not but halt and look back. There was no white thing framed in the hole of the gate, but there was a draped form shambling away among the trees …

Interestingly, local artist and writer Beryl Dyson learned that a particular room in the rectory was associated with nightmares and found that the story corresponded with a number of local features. This idea of the story reflecting a genuine experience was incorporated into a memorable documentary on M.R. James made by Anglia Television in 1995 in which Beryl Dyson participated.

The Most Haunted Village in England?

It is Beryl Dyson who has been responsible for researching and uncovering numerous accounts of ghosts in the village over two generations and it is from her books that the status of Great Livermere as the most haunted village in England has been established. Beryl Dyson's grandfather came to Livermere in the nineteenth century as an apprentice and, following his marriage in 1897, he settled and spent the rest of his life there. Beryl was born in the village and her first acquaintance with village ghosts came as a child of six or seven years old. As a child she herself saw a strange figure of a small man near the rectory gate. The experience made a lasting impression. In an interview in November 2001, Beryl Dyson described him as '… a little chap… he wore clothes a bit like a jester's, the collar had points on it and he had a shaven head and stood in front of me and grinned.' The small stature of the figure is reminiscent of many stories collected by folklorists in earlier generations concerning fairies and elfish creatures, particularly in the Celtic parts of the British Isles. In her own book Beryl Dyson admits, 'Even to this day, when passing that spot, I visualise that little man, with his grinning face, quite sure he was a ghost.'

Interestingly, she discovered that her experience occurred in the same spot where another villager saw two ghostly men sitting on a bench. A male spectre also haunts her cottage and has been heard easing himself into a particular chair.

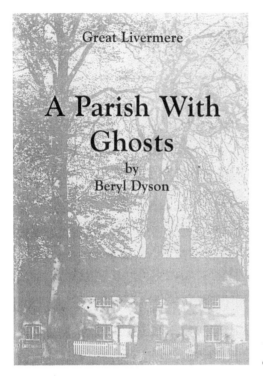

The cover of the first book by Beryl Dyson on the ghosts of Great Livermere.

Other ghosts recorded in Great Livermere by Beryl Dyson include:

1 A sensation of a presence of 'someone or something trying to push past' on a footpath through to the Village Hall and Callow Hill, past some allotments.

2 Two men in white smocks and old fashioned clothes seen sitting on a bench and walking across the paddock footpath to the church (at the same spot where Beryl had seen her small man as a child).

3 A ghostly black dog seen on the Thetford/Rhymer Road and on the Breck Road towards Ampton.

4 The phantom of an elderly lady seen in a cottage near the Mere.

5 A Grey Lady seen in a cottage by a seven-year-old-boy; footsteps and voices also heard in the house by the boy's mother in 1999 and 2000.

6 A 'ghostly wispy figure thought to be that of a woman' seen near the churchyard wall, typically seen by people out walking dogs, usually early in the morning.

7 Two phantom cyclists – a boy on a bicycle and the apparition of an older man on a penny-farthing. It seems possible that these two apparitions may be different aspects of a single haunting presence, the idea of a male cyclist which is manifested to witnesses in different guises.

8 A phantom car heard going through the park gates near Livermere Rectory at all hours of the day and night.

9 A 'wizened old man' in a broad brimmed hat seen by a reed cutter.

10 A monk like figure seen on the Bury to Great Barton Road, perhaps a former brother from Ixworth Priory.

11 A phantom lady in a hat seen in a cottage in Church Road by members of two different families.

12 A spot near the Livermere Park gates where dogs react with terror.

13 A lady in red seen on the road out to Thetford who acts in the tradition of 'spectral pedestrians' by appearing in the path of oncoming traffic and vanishing just as drivers think a collision is inevitable.

14 A pair of phantom horses ploughing in a field.

Taken together it appears that Great Livermere has at least fourteen documented ghosts. This exceeds the number claimed by the village of Pluckley, Kent, in its heyday in the late 1960s and early 1970s when it was celebrated as, 'the most the most haunted village in England'. Even Pluckley's pub sign was changed for a period to 'The Ghosts' in honour of the claim although the total figure for the number of ghosts was later substantially revised downwards.

In addition to these manifestations come a plethora of spirits reported by a spiritualist from a neighbouring village who has maintained he has had encounters with a wide range of presences, including a personality known as the headless man and a Roman lady who once occupied a villa in the parish, supposedly near the site of Livermere Rectory. A second book, *Friends, Romans and Ghosts* (2004), details some of these communications, maintaining a long tradition of spirit guides, a phenomena which has already been noted in different circumstances in respect of the communications recorded by the Revd Webling of Risby (see Chapter one). Because of the more subjective nature of these encounters it is harder to determine their essential nature, though both Beryl and her medium are convinced of the reality of these visions on some level. The communications are ongoing at the time of writing and a third book entitled *Great Livermere – A Community of Spirits* will appear in due course.

It can be cogently argued that to designate a place as the most haunted in England is to engage in an ultimately unprovable statistical exercise. Although some psychic researchers entertain the hypothesis of 'window areas' – locations which seem peculiarly prone to spontaneous psychic manifestations – their existence is incapable of conclusive demonstration. Indeed, their apparent existence may ultimately be only an artefact which reflects the diligent work of a local investigator or researcher who uncovers more psychic activity than an area without anyone to document experiences. Certainly, the credit for such an appellation must rest with the patient work that Beryl Dyson has undertaken over the years, documenting the experiences in her village. Other regions may be more haunted, but Great Livermere has been admirably served by Beryl Dyson who has recorded and preserved details of manifestations which otherwise would have been lost from memory in a few short years.

The gateway to Livermere Park.

Thus Great Livermere has more recorded ghosts than any other village of comparable size and population. Perhaps another key to its haunted quality is its relative isolation, even today. The experience of ghosts seems to arise in quiet, relaxed locations where the conscious mind has a chance to be at ease, free of distractions. For her part, Beryl Dyson identifies the Mere as one particularly numinous place, which has the capacity to inspire creativity and a personal sense of peace. Indeed, its tranquillity is little changed from when M.R. James wrote in a boyhood poem:

> Let me lie here beneath the waving fern
> Each eve above me shall the beetle hum
> From off the mere, above the oaks the hern
> Come sailing, and rooks fly calling home.

It may have been by such a sense of peace that M.R. James was inspired in 1899 to write words, in a letter of condolence to his friend James MacBryde, which reflected his optimistic and real faith in life after death, quite different from the tone of his stories:

I like to think – indeed it is more than thinking – that people when they go into the next world lose all their weakness and bodily trouble in which we have known them, and are young again and see the others whom they have been missing for a long time here, and are at their best, growing to be more perfect.

SELECT BIBLIOGRAPHY

Barker, H., *West Suffolk Illustrated* (1907)

Bardens, Dennis, *Ghosts and Hauntings* (1965)

Bury Free Pres: 1-15 March 1862; 1.3.46; 7.4.61; 12.5.61; 16.2.62; 23.9.66; 18.8.72; 1.8.75; 3.10.75; 7.4.78; 3.7.87; 10.11.89; 17.1.92; 2.4.99

Clarke, W.G., *In Breckland Wilds* (1925) Heffer & Sons Ltd

The Leader 21.2.80

Cox, Michael, *M.R. James: An Informal Portrait (*1983) OUP

Dyson, Beryl, *A Parish with Ghosts* (2001)

East Anglian Daily Times: 4.11.36; 20.9.67; 29.9.75; 17.12.75; 12.11.82; 25.2.89; 27.10.93. 5.12.96

Green, Andrew, *Our Haunted Kingdom* (1973) Wolfe

Halliday, Robert, *The Nichols Murder* in *Suffolk Review* (Spring 2001) No. 36 pp 19-29

Houghton, Bryan, *Saint Edmund King and Martyr* (1970) Terrence Dalton Ltd

Hopkins, R. Thurston, *Adventures with Phantoms* (1946); Ghosts over England (1953)

Jennett, Sean, *Suffolk and Essex* (1970) Travellers Guides Series, Darton, Longman and Todd

Mackintosh, Iain, *Pit, Boxes and Gallery – The Story of the Theatre Royal, Bury St Edmunds* (1979)

Orridge, John, *Description of the Gaol at Bury St Edmunds* (1819) London

Pfaff, Richard William, *Montague Rhodes James* (1980) Scolar Press, London

Porter, Enid, *The Folklore of East Anglia* (1974) Batsford

Prigg, Henry, *The Icklingham Papers* (1901)

Scott Davis, Alan and Greengrass, H., Ghosts *of Bury St Edmunds* (2000)

Thompson, Leonard, *Old Inns of Suffolk* (1946)

Turner, James, *Shrouds of Glory: Six Studies in Martyrdom* (1958).

Simpson, Jacqueline, '*The Rules of Folklore' in the Ghost Stories of M.R. James* in *Folklore* 108 (1997) 9-18

Society for Psychical Research File H104, Cambridge University Library

Underwood, Peter, *No Common Task* (1983)

Webling, A.F., *Risby* (1945) Edmund Ward

Webling, A.F., The *Two Brothers* (1948) Edmund Ward

West, H. Mills, *Ghosts of East Anglia* (1984) Countryside Books

Westley Parish Registrars

Yates, Richard, *History and Antiquities of the Abbey of Bury St. Edmunds*, 1820

Other local titles published by The History Press

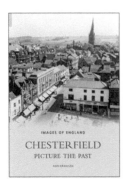

Chesterfield: Picture the Past
ANN KRAWSZIK

This collection of over 200 old photographs of Chesterfield is a sample of the many thousands of images which are now available to view on the award-winning website www.picturethepast.org.uk. These images, many never before published, provide a fascinating pictorial history of Chesterfield over the past 150 years. The result is a book that will delight anyone who has lived or worked in this popular market town with the leaning spire.

0 7524 3581 7

Buxton and the High Peak
MIKE LANGHAM, MIKE BENTLEY AND COLIN WELLS

Board's photographic business opened in the Devonshire Colonnade in the mid-1920s and when the firm closed in the 1970s its collection of glass-plate negatives was donated to the Buxton Museum for safe-keeping. This book is a second selection of images to be published from this valuable record of Buxton through the twentieth century and the choice of photographs has again been made by the local historians who compiled the first volume and who have been responsible for cataloguing the entire Board archive.

0 7524 3951 0

Sheffield Parks and Gardens
DOUGLAS HINDMARSH

Sheffield is justifiably proud of the parks, woodlands and open spaces which make it one of the greenest cities in Europe. However, in the early nineteenth century the town was overcrowded and polluted and there were no green spaces for leisure and recreation. This book illustrates how the parks and gardens were acquired and developed from the 1830s onwards, and shows some of the park features which have now disappeared. Also depicted are everyday events and special occasions such as Royal visits and Whitsuntide.

0 7524 3542 6

Belper and Milford
ADRIAN FARMER

From the eighteenth century to the present day, the cotton mill town of Belper and its smaller neighbour have reflected Britain's changing fortunes as an industrial nation – reaping the benefits of early innovations, only to lose so many of their industrial landmarks in the latter half of the twentieth century. Today the mills, along with much of both Belper and Milford, are part of the Derwent Valley Mills World Heritage Site.

0 7524 3376 8

If you are interested in purchasing other books published by The History Press, or in case you have difficulty finding any of our books in your local bookshop, you can also place orders directly through our website

www.thehistorypress.co.uk